YOUR BEAUTIFUL LIFE

D0547960

A GIFT

YOUR BEAUTIFUL LIFE

A GIFT

BRIAN SMYTH

Maybe International Publishing Division
6 The Commons, Fairyhouse Road, Ratoath, Co. Meath, Ireland

e-mail: info@maybeinternational.com
www.maybeinternational.com

Paperback ISBN: 978-0-9954628-0-9
Hardback: 978-0-9954628-1-6

Printed in England by CMP

James Connolly one of the leaders of the 1916 Easter uprising that led to Irish independence was wakened by a nurse on the night of the 11th of May to be told that he was to be executed at dawn.

His wife and daughter were informed and arrived to Kilmainham Jail at midnight.

"Well, Lillie, I suppose you know what this means?" Connolly said.
"Oh, James, it's not that - it's not that." his wife replied.

"Yes, Lillie. I fell asleep for the first time tonight and they wakened me at eleven and told me that I was to die at dawn."

His wife broke down and laid her head on the bed and sobbed heartbreakingly.

Connolly patted her head and said:
"Don't cry, Lillie, you'll unman me."

"But your beautiful life, James. Your beautiful life!" she sobbed.

"Well, Lillie, hasn't it been a full life and isn't this a good end?"

Dedication

I whole heartedly dedicate this book to the many, many people who manage each day to live beautiful lives. Most of these I have never known and never will. Some I have had and continue to have the joy of knowing. I thank you all.

One of these is Ximo Santoja from Alicante in Spain who designed this book.

If creativity, energy, good will, humour and infinite patience are part of leading a beautiful life, then Ximo's certainly is one.

Many thanks Ximo.

Welcome to *Your Beautiful Life* and welcome to the invitation to see and treat every day and every moment and experience in your life, as a wonderful gift.

There are two routes you can take to reading and using *Your Beautiful Life*

Route 1- Your Daily Reminder and Companion

Every day in our lives contains a rich bounty of many different gifts.

Sometimes it's hard to see them and sometimes we just can't.

Your Beautiful Life is intended to help you to be able to see those gifts, some of which can be difficult to spot because they come in the ordinary containers of 'ordinary' everyday events and happenings.

You will, of course, revisit each day 12 times in the year, but each visit will be different because you will be different each time, each month.

It's a wonderful life and I hope *Your Beautiful Life* helps you to see and feel that wonder as often as possible, every day, of every month, of every year.

I hope it does so especially when the wonder is hidden and you doubt that it is even there. It is. It always is.

Listen to: It's a Wonderful Life

SCAN WITH SMARTPHONE

Route 2 - Your Companion in the Events, Experiences, Moods and Emotions you Encounter in Life.

We go through many different experiences in the course of our lives, with accompanying moods and emotions.

Each day is a fresh opportunity to reflect on these and, on yourself and on what is happening, going on in your life.

It is easy to miss the messages that come our way each day speaking to us, calling to us, inviting us to pay attention and to be the best we can be so we make the most of our lives and wonderful world.

Your Beautiful Life is a companion to remind and help you make the most of the opportunity each day brings and to get in touch with whatever you are experiencing or feeling.

There are over 120 situations or experiences listed at the end of the book, pointing you to where that topic is mentioned.

Your Beautiful Life does not, of course, pretend to give answers for all of these experiences and feelings but invites you to explore and see them in a new, positive and life-filled light.

DAY 1

Whatever you can do or dream you can, begin it.
Boldness has genius, power and magic in it.
Begin it now.

Goethe

THEME
FOR TODAY

No matter where you are at or what has happened you can begin again today, start afresh. **WHAT IS ONE THING YOU WOULD LIKE TO MAKE A FRESH START ON?**

Is there anything you have been toying with or thinking of doing for a while? **BEGIN IT TODAY. WHY NOT!**

Can you recall the dreams and wishes and goals you had when you first started on the road you are now on? Feel like you felt then. **WHY NOT REVISIT THEM, RETURN TO THEM AND LIVE THEM?**

What is the one thing in your life that is more important than anything else? Have you been giving it enough focus and attention? IF NOT, BEGIN TODAY. **IT'S A GOOD DAY TO DO IT.**

Be alert for new things today. They will be there. **DON'T MISS THEM.**

We can get into routines, patterns, habits in our lives.

These can be quite comfortable places to be. They can also be places that blind us from seeing the wonderful things around us, and hold us back from doing far greater things that are more in line with who we really are and that the world needs from us.

Today is an invitation to begin again or to decide to begin something new. Listen to hear and heed the invitation today is giving you.

YOUR COMPANIONS TODAY
WHO WOULD YOU LIKE FOR COMPANY TODAY?
ALL THESE BEGAN THEIR LIVES ON THE FIRST DAY OF THE MONTH AND ARE AVAILABLE TO
ACCOMPANY YOU ON FRESH STARTS, ON NEW BEGINNINGS TODAY.

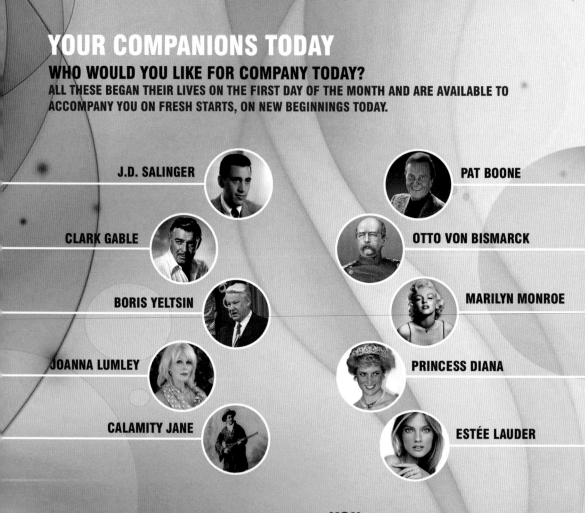

J.D. SALINGER

PAT BOONE

CLARK GABLE

OTTO VON BISMARCK

BORIS YELTSIN

MARILYN MONROE

JOANNA LUMLEY

PRINCESS DIANA

CALAMITY JANE

ESTÉE LAUDER

WHAT QUALITIES DO THEY HAVE THAT YOU WOULD LIKE TO HAVE?
WHAT QUALITIES DO YOU HAVE THAT YOU ARE EITHER NOT SUFFICIENTLY AWARE OF OR ARE NOT
PUTTING TO ENOUGH GOOD USE?
▷ ▷ ▷ ▷ ▷ ▷ ▷ HOW CAN YOU PRACTISE AND LIVE THESE TODAY? ▷ ▷ ▷

ONE OF THESE HAS A SPECIAL MESSAGE
FOR **YOU** TODAY.

WHO MIGHT IT BE?
WHAT MIGHT IT BE?

OPENING OUR EYES TO WHAT IS IMPORTANT AND TO WHAT IS:

A prisoner lived in solitary confinement for years.

He saw and spoke to no one and his meals were served through an opening in the wall.

One day an ant came into his cell.

The man contemplated it in fascination as it crawled around the room. He held it in the palm of his hand the better to observe it, gave it a grain or two of food to eat, and kept it under his tin cup at night.

One day it suddenly struck him that it had taken 10 long years of solitary confinement to open his eyes to the loveliness of an ant.

TASTE IT!

IF YOU ARE DRINKING A CUP OF TEA OR COFFEE TODAY, STOP BEFORE YOU BEGIN TO DRINK AND DECIDE TO APPRECIATE EVERY SIP.

IMAGINE IT IS YOUR VERY FIRST TIME TO DRINK TEA OR COFFEE. IMAGINE YOU WILL HAVE TO DESCRIBE TO SOMEONE WHAT DRINKING TEA OR COFFEE IS LIKE. ABOVE ALL, TASTE THE AFTER-TASTE.

**DON'T FORGET.
DON'T WASTE EVEN ONE SIP.**

First they came for the Communists
And I did not speak out
Because I was not a Communist
Then they came for the Socialists
And I did not speak out
Because I was not a Socialist
Then they came for the trade unionists
And I did not speak out
Because I was not a trade unionist
Then they came for the Jews
And I did not speak out
Because I was not a Jew
Then they came for me
And there was no one left
To speak out for me

Martin Niemoller

MANY PEOPLE BELIEVE THAT YOU ARE A SOUL ENCASED IN FLESH, SEPARATE FROM THE WORLD AND SEPARATE FROM OTHER SOULS.

BUT... MAYBE THIS IS NOT SO.

Maybe the truth is that Separateness is an illusion.

Oneness is the reality. You are as much one with everything else as the leaf is part of the tree and the tree part of its environment.

Why not act and live today as if THIS version is true. It will enrich everything you do and transform your day.

And....as a matter of fact...it IS true.

LISTEN TO

THE FIRST TIME EVER I SAW YOUR FACE
BY
THE TEMPTATIONS

SCAN WITH SMARTPHONE

On your way to or from work today, or wherever you are going, see something that you have never noticed before.

Wherever you see ONE thing on its own, smile.

Look at something on your desk or in your vicinity and see it as if you were seeing it for the first time.
Forget what it is or what you call it and see it 'for the first time' in a new way.

Who is the number ONE person for you in all of history?

Why are you the only ONE person who can fulfil YOUR mission, what you are called to do?

... from his book *It's a Dog's World!*

WHEN LOVED ONES COME HOME, ALWAYS RUN TO GREET THEM.

YOUR BRAIN TEASER FOR TODAY

A SNAIL IS AT THE BOTTOM OF A WELL 30 FEET DEEP. IT CAN CRAWL UPWARD 3 FEET IN ONE DAY, BUT AT NIGHT IT SLIPS BACK 2 FEET.

HOW LONG DOES IT TAKE THE SNAIL TO CRAWL OUT OF THE WELL?

YOUR
MANAGEMENT
MESSAGE
FOR
TODAY
IS

I always find it amusing that managers will say they want themselves and their people to be successful but not necessarily happy.

"We might make a few people happy if possible", they say, "and if it happens, well and good. But we certainly don't aim to make everyone happy, or even the vast majority of people who work for us. If we do manage to make them happy, it's a by-product, incidental".

How sad! We are capable of more and deserving of more.

Managing to be Human p. 10

LEADING BUSINESS ORGANISATIONS
WITH INTEGRITY AND EFFECTIVENESS

MANAGING
TO BE
HUMAN

BRIAN F. SMYTH

New Every Morning

Every day is a fresh beginning
Listen my soul to the glad refrain
And, spite of old sorrows
And older sinning
Troubles forecasted
And possible pain
Take heart with the day and begin
again

Susan Coolidge

END OF DAY

THINK OF ONE THING YOU FEEL PLEASED AND PROUD ABOUT TODAY.

WHAT IS ONE THING YOU LEARNED TODAY OR REALIZED FOR THE FIRST TIME?

WHAT IS ONE THING YOU CHANGED OR THAT YOU BEGAN TODAY, OR THAT YOU DECIDED YOU WILL BEGIN?

WHAT IS ONE THING YOU SAW IN A NEW AND FRESH WAY TODAY THAT YOU HAD NOT NOTICED BEFORE?

DAY 2

DREAM BIG

The African model of leadership is better expressed as 'Ubuntu', the idea that people are empowered by other people, that we become our best selves through unselfish interaction with others.

Nelson Mandela

WELCOME TO THE 2nd GREAT DAY
YOU CAN LEARN LOTS OF THINGS TODAY, IF YOU WANT!

YOU CAN LEARN TO PAY ATTENTION TO THE OTHER PERSON YOU ARE WITH

YOU CAN LEARN TO NOT ALWAYS BE FIRST OR TO NEED TO BE

YOU CAN LEARN TO RELY ON AND TO TRUST OTHERS

YOU CAN LEARN TO SERVE AND TO HELP OTHERS

OK? WHICH WILL YOU GO AFTER TODAY SO YOU USE THIS GREAT DAY TO GROW AND TO LIVE?

TO ACCOMPANY YOU ON THIS GREAT DAY AND ON ALL THE LEARNINGS YOU WILL GET YOU HAVE:

BRITNEY SPEARS

MIKHAIL GORBACHEV

MARIA CALLAS

DANIEL BOONE

THERESE DE LISIEUX

LES DAWSON

DR. SEUSS

BURT LANCASTER

JAMES JOYCE

HERMAN HESSE

ALL OF THESE WANT TO BE WITH YOU TODAY AND BELIEVE THEY CAN HELP YOU TO MAKE IT A GREAT DAY. WHO WILL YOU CHOOSE? AND REMEMBER YOU CAN CHOOSE SOMEONE DIFFERENT EACH MONTH DEPENDING ON HOW YOU FEEL.

WHAT QUALITIES DO THESE PEOPLE HAVE THAT YOU WOULD LIKE TO HAVE?
WHAT QUALITIES DO YOU HAVE THAT YOU ARE EITHER NOT SUFFICIENTLY AWARE OF OR ARE NOT PUTTING TO ENOUGH GOOD USE?
HOW CAN YOU PRACTISE AND LIVE THESE TODAY?

BE WATCHFUL FOR OTHER PEOPLE TODAY.
THERE ARE PEOPLE AROUND YOU WHO NEED YOU BUT MAY NOT SAY OR SHOW IT.

A rich lady stepped out of a fashionable hotel in London where she had been dining and dancing all evening at a charity ball in aid of street urchins. She was about to get into her Rolls Royce when a street urchin approached her and asked her for sixpence saying he hadn't eaten for two days.

"You ungrateful wretch", the woman shouted at him.

"Don't you realize I have been eating and dancing for you all night?"

He who binds to himself a joy
Does the winged life destroy;
But he who kisses the joy as it flies
Lives in eternity s sun rise.

William Blake

TWO ROADS DIVERGED IN A YELLOW WOOD,
AND SORRY I COULD NOT TRAVEL BOTH
AND BE ONE TRAVELER, LONG I STOOD
AND LOOKED DOWN ONE AS FAR AS I COULD
TO WHERE IT BENT IN THE UNDERGROWTH;

THEN TOOK THE OTHER, AS JUST AS FAIR,
AND HAVING PERHAPS THE BETTER CLAIM,
BECAUSE IT WAS GRASSY AND WANTED WEAR;
THOUGH AS FOR THAT THE PASSING THERE
HAD WORN THEM REALLY ABOUT THE SAME,

AND BOTH THAT MORNING EQUALLY LAY
IN LEAVES NO STEP HAD TRODDEN BLACK.
OH, I KEPT THE FIRST FOR ANOTHER DAY!
YET KNOWING HOW WAY LEADS ON TO WAY,
I DOUBTED IF I SHOULD EVER COME BACK.

I SHALL BE TELLING THIS WITH A SIGH
SOMEWHERE AGES AND AGES HENCE:
TWO ROADS DIVERGED IN A WOOD, AND I -
I TOOK THE ONE LESS TRAVELED BY,
AND THAT HAS MADE ALL THE DIFFERENCE.

ROBERT FROST

TODAY
LOOK FOR THINGS IN PAIRS.
SPOT ANY TWO THINGS TOGETHER.

BIRDS
PEOPLE
DOGS
TREES
HOUSES

ANY TWO THINGS AND SEE HOW
THEY LIKE BEING TOGETHER

SMELL TWO PERFUMES
OR COLOGNES TODAY
AND NOTE HOW
THEY DIFFER

A little girl was dying of a disease from which her eight-year-old brother had recovered some time before. The doctor said to the boy, "Only a transfusion of your blood will save the life of your sister. Are you ready to give her your blood?"

The eyes of the boy widened in fear. He hesitated for a while, then finally said, "Okay, doctor. I'll do it."

An hour after the transfusion was completed the boy asked hesitantly, "Say, Dr, when do I die?"

It was only then that the doctor understood the momentary fear that had seized the child: he thought that in giving his blood he was giving his life for his sister.

A Poison Tree

I was angry with my friend;
I told my wrath, my wrath did end.
I was angry with my foe:
I told it not, my wrath did grow.

And I watered it in fears,
Night & morning with my tears:
And I sunned it with smiles,
And with soft deceitful wiles.

And it grew both day and night.
Till it bore an apple bright.
And my foe beheld it shine,
And he knew that it was mine.

And into my garden stole,
When the night had veild the pole;
In the morning glad I see;
My foe outstretched beneath the tree.

William Blake

... from his book *It's a Dog's World!*

THINK OF HOW MANY PEOPLE YOU CAN MAKE HAPPY IN A DAY - JUST BY HOW YOU ARE.

YOUR BRAIN TEASER FOR TODAY

A missionary visits an island where two tribes live. One tribe always tells the truth. The other always lies. The truth tellers live on the western side of the island and the liars live on the eastern side of the island. The missionary's problem is to determine who tells the truth by asking one native only one question.

The missionary, seeing a native walking in the distance, asks a nearby native: "Go ask that native in the distance which side of the island he lives on."

When the messenger returns he answers: "He says he lives on the western side of the island."

Is the messenger a truth teller or a liar? How can you be sure?

24

YOUR
MANAGEMENT
MESSAGE
FOR
TODAY
IS

'When we come across a so-called 'difficult person', we are really talking about how we feel, of the effect or impact of that person on us. We are feeling something and attributing the cause of that feeling to how another person is behaving.

These people are expressing some need and maybe not doing so in a very helpful way.

What is called for is a good reading of what it is the person needs and some understanding of why they are the way they are.

If we can help them to be more human we, ourselves, will become more human in the process.'

DING BUSINESS ORGANISATIONS
TH INTEGRITY AND EFFECTIVENESS

MANAGING
TO BE
HUMAN

BRIAN F. SMYTH

END OF DAY

WHAT ARE TWO THINGS YOU DID REALLY WELL TODAY?

WHAT TWO LEARNINGS DID YOU GET ...ABOUT LIFE OR ABOUT YOURSELF?

THINK OF TWO PEOPLE YOU LOVE AND TWO PEOPLE YOU BELIEVE LOVE YOU.

WHO DID YOU MANAGE TO SEE IN A NEW LIGHT TODAY?

WHO DID YOU HELP, IF EVEN IN A SMALL WAY?

DAY 3

"I feel myself so much a part of everything living that I am not the least concerned with the beginning or ending of the concrete existence of any one person in this eternal flow."

Albert Einstein

You are connected to everything and everyone else. They are part of you and you form part of them. Enjoy your mutual interdependence today.

WELCOME TO THE 3rd GREAT DAY.
YOU CAN LEARN LOTS OF THINGS TODAY, IF YOU WANT!

THINK OF THREE PEOPLE WHO 'DEPEND' ON YOU AND THREE PEOPLE ON WHOM YOU 'DEPEND'.

SEE – OR NOTICE – TREES WHEREVER YOU GO TODAY.

ENJOY THEIR UNIQUENESS, AND NOT ONLY IN THE TREE ITSELF, BUT REMEMBER THAT EVERY ONE OF THE -ON AVERAGE- 200,000 LEAVES ON EVERY TREE IS DIFFERENT FROM EVERY OTHER LEAF…AND SO ON FOR EVERY OTHER TREE.

HOW ARE YOU UNIQUE?

WHAT IS YOUR UNIQUE QUALITY, GIFT, ATTRIBUTE THAT NOBODY ELSE HAS?

HOW CAN YOU DEVELOP AND PUT THIS UNIQUENESS TO WORK FOR YOURSELF AND FOR THE WORLD?

IF A LEAF CAN DO IT, SO CAN YOU!

THINK OF EXAMPLES OF THREES. THERE ARE LOTS OF THEM…APART FROM THE POOR BLIND MICE!

Trees

I think that I shall never see
A poem lovely as a tree.

A tree whose hungry mouth is prest
Against the earth's sweet flowing breast;

A tree that looks at God all day,
And lifts her leafy arms to pray;

A tree that may in Summer wear
A nest of robins in her hair;

Upon whose bosom snow has lain;
Who intimately lives with rain.

Poems are made by fools like me,
But only God can make a tree.

Joyce Kilmeer

While every tree looks symmetrical from a distance, underneath or within it you will see that all the branches are twisted and turned in all kinds of directions in their search for light.
Yet every tree ends up coordinated, beautiful.

What are some twists and turns and forced changes you have experienced in your life? Can you understand and be grateful for them, difficult as they were at the time, because they have led you to your present symmetry? **BE** grateful.

Trees are models of cooperation and collaboration
– with their whole environment –
interacting, accommodating, adjusting, tolerating, contributing.

Check how well you do this because it is what will give you your greatest strength and stability and groundedness.

IN WORKING WITH OTHERS AND IN STRIVING TO DO SO WELL IN YOUR OWN UNIQUE WAY YOU HAVE MANY FRIENDS WHO WANT TO HELP YOU. CHOOSE WHO YOU WANT TO HELP YOU TODAY.

YOU CAN VARY YOUR CHOICE EACH TIME ROUND, EACH MONTH, BASED ON HOW YOU FEEL AND WHAT YOU NEED.

TONY CURTIS

NICCOLO MACHIAVELLI

RAUL CASTRO

BING CROSBY

COLIN MEADS

SUGAR RAY ROBINSON

MARLON BRANDO

BEN ELTON

FRANZ KAFKA

MARTIN SHEEN

WHAT QUALITIES DO THEY HAVE THAT YOU WOULD LIKE TO HAVE?
WHAT QUALITIES DO YOU HAVE THAT YOU ARE EITHER NOT SUFFICIENTLY AWARE OF OR ARE NOT PUTTING TO ENOUGH GOOD USE?
HOW CAN YOU PRACTISE AND LIVE THESE TODAY?

SOME PEOPLE BELIEVE THAT OUR DESTINY IS TO COMPLETE THE CONQUEST OF NATURE: TO FREE OURSELVES FROM LABOUR, FROM DISEASE, FROM DEATH ITSELF, TO ASCEND TO THE STARS AND LEAVE NATURE BEHIND

BUT..MAYBE THIS IS NOT SO.

Maybe the truth is that we do not want to flee or get away from mother earth but see it as where we have come from and what we belong to, seeing our destinies as united and one, and trusting in the 'laws' of life and death that operate in our exciting home.

Why not act and live today as if THIS version is true. It will enrich everything you do and transform your day.

And….as a matter of fact…it IS true.

LISTEN TO

THIRD MOVEMENT FROM SYMPHONY NO. 3
BY
BEETHOVEN

SCAN WITH SMARTPHONE

At some point today, take 3 minutes to be quiet and to stop thinking and just BE.

LISTEN TO THE SILENCE

Notice any intruding thoughts.
Try to locate a three-legged stool today and sit on it and enjoy doing so.
Go for a walk where there are trees and see if you can see three of them together.

BEING SPECIAL CAN HAVE ITS PROBLEMS

Goldstein, aged 92, had lived through pogroms in Poland, concentration camps in Germany and dozens of other persecutions against the Jews.

"Oh, Lord!" he said, "Isn't it true that we are your chosen people?"

A Heavenly voice replied. "Yes, Goldstein, the Jews are my chosen people."

"Well, then, isn't it time you chose somebody else?"

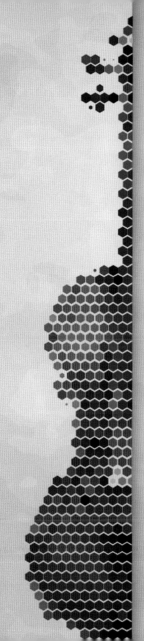

Ode

We are the music-makers,
And we are the dreamers of dreams,
Wandering by lone sea-breakers
And sitting by desolate streams;
World losers and world forsakers,
On whom the pale moon gleams:
Yet we are the movers and shakers
Of the world for ever, it seems.

With wonderful deathless ditties
We build up the world's great cities.
And out of a fabulous story
We fashion an empire's glory:
One man with a dream, at pleasure,
Shall go forth and conquer a crown;
And three with a new song's measure
Can trample an empire down.

We, in the ages lying
In the buried past of the earth,
Built Nineveh with our sighing,
And Babel itself with our mirth;
And o'erthrew them with prophesying
To the old of the new world's worth;
For each age is a dream that is dying,
Or one that is coming to birth.

Arthur O Shaughnessy

SIMBA'S
TIP FOR TODAY

ALLOW THE EXPERIENCE OF FRESH AIR AND THE WIND IN YOUR FACE TO BE PURE ECSTASY

YOUR BRAIN
TEASER FOR TODAY

ONLY THREE BOXES

Three boxes are labelled 'Apples', 'Oranges' and 'Apples and Oranges'.

Each label is incorrect.

You may select only one fruit from one box. (No feeling around or peeking permitted!).

How can you label each box correctly?

YOUR MANAGEMENT MESSAGE FOR TODAY IS

A manager has the responsibility and privilege to help people in three ways:

To help them to KNOW what is expected of them and what they need to do.

To help them to WANT to do what they are required to do.

To help them to be ABLE to do what their job or role entails.

Every person who has a problem will fall into one of these three categories:

1. *They don't KNOW they have a problem.*

2. *They do know but don't WANT to do anything about it.*

3. *They know there is a problem, want to do something about it but are not ABLE.*

BUILDING BUSINESS ORGANISATIONS
WITH INTEGRITY AND EFFECTIVENESS

MANAGING TO BE HUMAN

BRIAN F. SMYTH

END OF DAY

WHAT THINGS BLOCKED YOUR WAY TO THE LIGHT TODAY? HOW DID YOU HANDLE THEM?

THINK OF THREE PEOPLE YOU SPOKE TO TODAY AND REVIEW HOW WELL YOU HANDLED THE CONVERSATIONS.

WHAT IS ONE THING YOU DID TODAY THAT SHOWS HOW UNIQUE YOU ARE?

FEEL THE PLEASURE OF BELONGING TO SOMETHING GREATER AND TO A NETWORK OF GREAT PEOPLE.

DAY 4

It's four in the morning, a difficult hour for humanity. It is a time when one's conscious defences are down, when one is physically most vulnerable, prey to brooding and regrets, to dark thoughts.

Deirdre Madden

Yes, night can be a dark time in various senses and we can feel alone and insecure. But this is only because we can't see how strong and supported we really are and how strong and supportive we can be for others. Today you can feel grateful for all the supports around you and for the great strengths, deep within you.

FOR THIS REASON,
IT IS IMPORTANT TO GET THE DAY OFF TO A GOOD START SO:

Think of four nice and good friends you have.

Think of four reasons to be happy.

Think of four achievements in your life to date.

Think of four things that you are excited about.

What are four solid things in your life at present?
Four bases or foundations that are real supports in your life?
Start with yourself and your own gifts!

OK NOW?   IN CASE YOU AWOKE AT 4 A.M.!

The breezes at dawn have secrets to tell you
Don't go back to sleep!
You must ask for what you really want.
Don't go back to sleep!
People are going back and forth
across the doorsill where the two worlds touch,
The door is round and open
Don't go back to sleep!"

Rumi

Today should be about confidence and belief.
You can be a great support to people around you by the strength of your confidence and by the strength of your resolve and determination.
Today, think of four or more people who depend on you, who look to you, even if they never say or admit it.
Be strong for these people.
And be strong because you **ARE** strong.

WHAT ARE FOUR STRENGTHS THAT YOU BELIEVE YOU HAVE?

WHAT FOUR STRENGTHS DO OTHERS SEE YOU HAVE?

YOU ARE NOT ALONE IN YOUR EFFORTS TO BE STRONG FOR PEOPLE. YOU HAVE SOME GREAT ALLIES WHO WERE BORN ON THIS DAY

ANTHONY PERKINS

BEYONCE KNOWLES

BRUCE DERN

LOUIS SATCHMO ARMSTRONG

BOB CHAMPION

MAYA ANGELOU

NEIL SIMON

JOHN LANDY

TOM WATSON

FRANCISCO FRANCO

ALL HAVE EXPRESSED THEIR SUPPORT FOR YOU SO CHOOSE ONE OR TWO WHOSE QUALITIES AND STRENGTHS YOU NEED OR WOULD LIKE TO HAVE TODAY.

WHAT QUALITIES DO THEY HAVE THAT YOU WOULD LIKE TO HAVE?
WHAT QUALITIES DO YOU HAVE THAT YOU ARE EITHER NOT SUFFICIENTLY AWARE OF OR ARE NOT PUTTING TO ENOUGH GOOD USE?
HOW CAN YOU PRACTISE AND LIVE THESE TODAY?

Holding out in hope:

An ancient king in India sentenced a man to death.

The man begged that the sentence be condoned, and added, "If the King will be merciful and spare my life, I shall teach his horse to fly in a year's time."

"Done," said the King.

"But if at the end of this period the horse cannot fly, you will be executed."

When his anxious family later asked the man how he planned to achieve this, he said, "In the course of the year the king may die.

Or the horse may die.

Or who knows, the horse may learn to

Oh, life is a glorious cycle of song,
A medley of extemporanea;
And love is a thing that can never go wrong;
And I am Marie of Roumania.

Dorothy Parker

NOTICE THINGS WITH FOUR ASPECTS TO THEM – TABLES, CHAIRS, ROOMS, CARS ETC.

EVERY ONE YOU SPOT WILL GIVE YOU STRENGTH AND SOLIDITY AND CONFIDENCE TO BE AS STRONG AS YOU NEED TO BE TODAY.

WHAT DOES 'FOUR' MEAN TO YOU? ANY STORIES WITH 4 IN THEM? MYTHS?

REALLY AWARE

An old man lived most of his life on what was considered to be one of the loveliest islands in the world.

Now that he had returned to spend his retirement years in the big city, someone said to him, "It must have been wonderful to live for so many years on an island that is considered one of the wonders of the world."

The old man gave it some thought, then said,
"Well, to tell you the truth, if I'd known it was so famous, I'd have looked at it."

Are YOU looking at YOUR island?

THERE IS A BELIEF THAT INTELLIGENCE, ORDER, PURPOSE AND DESIGN ARE ILLUSIONS; UNDERNEATH IT ALL IS MERELY A PURPOSELESS JUMBLE OF FORCES AND MASSES.

BUT there are many mystics and physicists who claim that it is not so and that there is a beautiful intelligence at work in and through everything, including you, drawn towards the fulfilment of a higher purpose.

Can you feel what they are saying and spot and live out this intelligence that is at work in you and in everything today?

LISTEN TO

COUNTDOWN

BY

BEYONCE'S ALBUM 4

SCAN WITH SMARTPHONE

Happy the man, and happy he alone,
He who can call today his own:
He who, secure within, can say,
Tomorrow do thy worst, for I have lived today.
Be fair or foul or rain or shine,
The joys I have possessed, in spite of fate, are mine.
Not Heaven itself upon the past has power,
But what has been, has been, and I have had my hour.

John Dryden

SIMBA'S
TIP FOR TODAY

... from his book: *It's a Dog's Life I hope?*

WHEN IT'S IN YOUR BEST
INTERESTS, PRACTISE OBEDIENCE

(SIMBA AND THOMAS AQUINAS ARE NOT
IN FULL AGREEMENT ON EVERYTHING!)

YOUR BRAIN
TEASER FOR TODAY

A LOVE STORY....A LOVE RECTANGLE!

One of your staff, Arthur, has not been working well lately and seems upset and down. He works in a department with seven other single people, three men and four women.

They socialise a lot and it seems that each one has fallen in love with one other person and is himself/herself loved by one other person. John falls in love with a girl who is unfortunately in love with Jim. Arthur loves a girl who loves a man who loves Ellen.

Mary is loved by the man who is loved by the girl, who is loved by Bruce. Gloria hates Bruce and is hated by the man whom Hazel loves. Who loves poor Arthur?

Maybe she can help you get Arthur back working well again!

YOUR
MANAGEMENT
MESSAGE
FOR
TODAY
IS

LEADING BUSINESS ORGANISATIONS
WITH INTEGRITY AND EFFECTIVENESS

MANAGING
TO BE
HUMAN

BRIAN F. SMYTH

"A Company (cum pan – with bread) can be a wonderful source of interest and meaning for people, supporting them in every aspect of their lives.

What a great help you can be to people as a manager! What has happened is that work and culture have become separated to the detriment of both. This comes from the emphasis on the individual at the expense of the communal.

The latter, the communal is merely a possible and vocational support for the former, the individual, who is primordial. It is all about me as an individual, as an isolated, independent and stand-alone individual person or company."

END OF DAY

WHO DID YOU HELP TODAY?

WHAT STRENGTHS DID YOU DISCOVER IN YOURSELF TODAY? WHAT STRENGTHS WOULD YOU LIKE TO HAVE OR TO DEVELOP?

WHO ARE THE OTHER THREE LEGS ON YOUR TABLE ON WHOM YOU DEPEND AND WHO DEPEND ON YOU?
WHICH OF THESE MOST NEEDS YOUR SUPPORT AND STRENGTH?

WHO DID YOU HELP AND SUPPORT TODAY?

DAY 5

When a friend makes a mistake,
the mistake is still a mistake
And the friend is still a friend

Shimon Peres

REAL FRIENDSHIP AND TRUST!

The old miser was overheard at his prayers: "If the Almighty, may His holy name be blessed forever, would give me $100,000, I would give $10,000 to the poor.

I promise I would. And if the Almighty, may He be glorified forever, were not to trust me, let Him deduct $10,000 in advance and just send me the balance."

Trusting has to be done unilaterally.

TODAY IS A DAY OF FRIENDSHIP FOR YOU

"My friend isn't back from the battlefield, sir. Request permission to go out and get him."

"Permission refused," said the officer. "I don't want you to risk your life for a man who is probably dead."

The soldier went, all the same, and, an hour later came back mortally wounded, carrying the corpse of his friend.

The officer was furious.

"I told you he was dead. Now I will lose both of you. Tell me, was it worth going out there to bring in a corpse?"

"Oh, yes, It was, sir", the dying man replied. "When I got to him he was still alive. And he said to me, 'Jack, I knew you'd come.'"

49

LOTS OF FRIENDS TO KEEP YOU COMPANY TODAY!

GUY DE MAUPASSANT

JOHN HUSTON

NEIL ARMSTRONG

SAMANTHA SANG

JESSE JAMES

NEIL ARMSTRONG

RAQUEL WELCH

FREDDY MERCURY

GEORGE WASHINGTON

WALT DISNEY

COULDN'T GO WRONG WITH SOME OF THESE.
BUT DON'T CHOOSE THEM ALL. KEEP SOME FOR NEXT MONTH!

WHAT QUALITIES DO THEY HAVE THAT YOU WOULD LIKE TO HAVE?
WHAT QUALITIES DO YOU HAVE THAT YOU ARE EITHER NOT SUFFICIENTLY AWARE OF OR ARE NOT
PUTTING TO ENOUGH GOOD USE?
HOW CAN YOU PRACTISE AND LIVE THESE TODAY?

POEM FOR FIVE FRIENDS

O my Five Friends whom I won out of the indifferent
Crowds rushing to their appointed stations
It is autumning again over my Pembrokeshire
And I need more than ever the consolations
Of those who care like prayer; with easy eyes
Smoothe down the jittery nerves; with unselfish ears
Deliver a friend's message into time
Give him hope and home and family ties
What never he did have through all his years
O my Five Friends pray with me to the end of the rhyme
And I will in your name absorb
The poignancy of the yellow leaves coming down again
And I who thought that before now I would disturb
The relentless cycle of my character
And live beautifully as God promised me
Walk down Pembroke Road alone
Still dragging on his cursed predestined chain
O my Five friends O my Five Friends
Thank you ever so much for all you've done.

Patrick Kavanagh

FIND YELLOW EVERYWHERE YOU GO TODAY AND LET IT WARM YOU LIKE THE SUN AND LET IT MAKE YOU SMILE.

EAT A BANANA TODAY AND ADMIRE IT BEFORE YOU OPEN IT AND SAVOUR EVERY BITE.

JUST DO IT...
UNLESS YOU HAVE AN
ALLERGY TO BANANAS
OR TO YELLOW!

EVERYTHING THAT IS NOT SELF IS AT BEST INDIFFERENT TO OUR WELL-BEING, AT WORST HOSTILE.

Maybe everything IS part of, one with everything else and wants to contribute to the welfare of the whole and so to your welfare.

MAYBE everything wants to be friendly to you and to be your friend.

Why not act and live today as if THIS version is true.

It will enrich everything you do and transform your day.

And....as a matter of fact...it IS true.

LISTEN TO

TAKE 5
BY
DAVE BRUBECK

DON'T GO IN FRONT OF ME,
I MAY NOT FOLLOW.
DON'T COME BEHIND ME,
I MAY NOT LEAD.
WALK BESIDE ME AND BE MY FRIEND.

SIMBA'S
TIP FOR TODAY

... from his book: *I believe it's a Dog's life*

LET OTHERS KNOW WHEN THEY'VE INVADED YOUR TERRITORY

YOUR BRAIN
TEASER FOR TODAY

A friend of yours who is vice president of a large corporation had an extremely efficient housekeeper. When he left for his vacation, he instructed her to forward the mail to him at his camp. During July he received no mail, so he phoned his home and asked the housekeeper what had happened. She explained that he had forgotten to leave her the mailbox key.

Your friend, the vice president, being the nice man he is, apologised and promised to mail her the key right away. During August, he still received no mail, though the housekeeper had told him there was a batch of mail in the box. When he returned home, he told his housekeeper that she was disobedient and unreliable and fired her.

Was your friend right to do this or was he unfair?

The friends you have!!

YOUR
MANAGEMENT
MESSAGE
FOR
TODAY
IS

See how powerful you are and the enormous effects you can have and are having on the people around you.

Think of people who had great influences on you in your life – people who believed in you, who gave you a chance, who cared for you and gave you attention.

So, in terms of changing anything, you are immensely more powerful than you might have thought you were. You can have enormous effects on people all around you with whom you are connected. You can have enormous power through your relationships and it is a great responsibility to be in a position of influence at the centre of a network of relationships.

As managers, we have to take ourselves very seriously, in terms of how truly important we are to others and in how powerful we can be in influencing or changing the world, whatever that means for each of us and for you.

DING BUSINESS ORGANISATIONS
TH INTEGRITY AND EFFECTIVENESS

MANAGING
TO BE
HUMAN

BRIAN F. SMYTH

END OF DAY

DID YOU THINK OF ANY FRIENDS THAT NEED YOU OR NEED MORE FROM YOU?

SAY THANKS TO SOME OF YOUR DEAREST FRIENDS IN YOUR HEAD …AND TO YOUR GREATEST FRIEND OF ALL – LIFE…OR WHATEVER YOU CALL IT.

RESOLVE TO CALL OR TALK TO SOME FRIEND OF YOURS TOMORROW TO LET THEM KNOW HOW MUCH YOU APPRECIATE THEM…EVEN IF YOU DON'T SAY THAT.

DAY 6

Beauty is truth and truth beauty, that is all ye know on earth and all ye need to know. Beauty has its own authority.

Keats

Today you will find beauty and deep meaning in the ordinary things around you, the commonplace.

Even if there is no such thing!

In every place you are today, you have to identify some commonplace thing and examine and appreciate it for what it is.

Any time you are feeling down, accept it and live with it and don't seek to get away from it, to flee it. Stay with your 'downess'. It is ok. BE there. It will pass. But don't want or wait for it to pass. It's an ok place to be.

Your challenge – and your invitation – will be to enjoy the ordinary and routine things in your day, the chores, the things you pay little attention to or that you dismiss or get out of the way as fast as you can.

Pay attention to what is on the ground, on the earth – floors, footpaths, roads, fields, lawns, soil, gardens, carpets, tiles and feel the life in them.

Every thing you do today, do it with meaning and feeling, however 'ordinary' you perceive it. Give it your full attention.

SEEING WHAT IS REALLY IN FRONT OF YOU

A guru asked his disciples how they could tell when the night had ended and the day begun.

One said, "When you see an animal in the distance and can tell whether it is a cow or a horse."

"No," said the Guru.

"When you look at a tree in the distance and can tell if it is a neem tree or a mango tree." Another disciple answered.

"Wrong again," said the guru.

"Well, then, what is it?" asked the disciples.

"When you look into the face of any man and recognise your brother in him; when you look into the face of any woman and recognise in her your sister. If you cannot do this, no matter at what time it is by the sun, it is still night."

Barter

Life has loveliness to sell,
All beautiful and splendid things,
Blue waves whitened on a cliff,
Soaring fire that sways and sings,
And children's faces looking up
Holding wonder like a cup.

Life has loveliness to sell,
Music like a curve of gold,
Scent of pine trees in the rain,
Eyes that love you, arms that hold,
And for your spirit's still delight,
Holy thoughts that star the night.

Spend all you have for loveliness,
Buy it and never count the cost;
For one white singing hour of peace
Count many a year of strife well lost,
And for a breath of ecstasy
Give all you have been, or could be.

Sara Teasdale

YOU HAVE SOME GREAT DOWN-TO-EARTH FRIENDS WITH YOU TODAY

LUCILLE BALL

MATEO RICCI

ALFRED TENNYSON

BUDDY HOLLY

DANIEL O´CONNELL

BRITT EKLAND

ANDY WARHOL

GERRY ADAMS

SYLVESTER STALLONE

GARY PLAYER

ANY ONE OF THESE WILL HELP TO KEEP YOU GROUNDED AND ENJOYING AND CELEBRATING THE SO-CALLED ORDINARY.

WHAT QUALITIES DO THEY HAVE THAT YOU WOULD LIKE TO HAVE?
WHAT QUALITIES DO YOU HAVE THAT YOU ARE EITHER NOT SUFFICIENTLY AWARE OF OR ARE NOT PUTTING TO ENOUGH GOOD USE?
HOW CAN YOU PRACTISE AND LIVE THESE TODAY?

SOME SAY THAT YOU ARE A BUBBLE OF PSYCHOLOGY, A MIND SEPARATE FROM OTHER MINDS AND SEPARATE FROM MATTER.

MAYBE THAT IS NOT SO AT ALL.

Maybe you are the product of, part of, matter which, like you, is spiritual to its core.

You share this union with everyone and everything else as together you continue to evolve to completion and fullness.

Why not act and live today as if THIS version is true.

It will enrich everything you do and transform your day.

And….as a matter of fact…it IS true.

LISTEN TO
FEET ON THE GROUND
BY
NINA RYNE

SCAN WITH SMARTPHONE

TO SEE A WORLD...
(Fragments from "Auguries of Innocence")

To see a World in a Grain of Sand
And a Heaven in a Wild Flower,
Hold Infinity in the palm of your hand
And Eternity in an hour.
A Robin Redbreast in a Cage
Puts all Heaven in a Rage.
A dove house fill'd with doves and pigeons
Shudders Hell thro' all its regions.

A Dog starv'd at his Master's Gate
Predicts the ruin of the State.
A Horse misus'd upon the Road
Calls to Heaven for Human blood.

Each outcry of the hunted Hare
A fiber from the Brain does tear.
The poison of the Snake and Newt
Is the sweat of Envy's Foot.

A truth that's told with bad intent
Beats all the Lies you can invent.
It is right it should be so;
Man was made for Joy and Woe;
And when this we rightly know
Thro' the World we safely go.

Every Night and every Morn
Some to Misery are Born.
Every Morn and every Night
Some are Born to sweet delight.

William Blake

THE 6 IS CONSIDERED THE MOST HARMONIOUS OF ALL SINGLE-DIGIT NUMBERS, IT IS NOT WITHOUT ITS FLAWS AND UPSETS. THE MOST IMPORTANT INFLUENCE OF THE 6 IS ITS LOVING AND CARING NATURE.

PROPERLY NICKNAMED THE MOTHERHOOD NUMBER, IT IS ALL ABOUT SACRIFICING, CARING, HEALING, PROTECTING AND TEACHING OTHERS.

NO FAMILY OR COMMUNITY CAN FUNCTION WITHOUT THE POWER OF THE 6 TO KEEP THEM TOGETHER AND SAFE. SHE IS THE GLUE THAT KEEPS A FAMILY OR COMMUNITY TOGETHER.

... from his book: *Believe it - It's a Dog's life*

I HAVE LIVED WITH MANY ZEN MASTERS, ALL OF THEM CATS!

YOUR BRAIN TEASER FOR TODAY

A woman goes into a hardware store to buy something for her house.

She asks the clerk the price, and the clerk replies: 'The price of one is twelve cents, the price of thirty is twentyfour cents, and the price of a hundred and forty four is thirty six cents.

What was the woman seeking to buy?

YOUR
MANAGEMENT
MESSAGE
FOR
TODAY
IS

"We are so accustomed to aiming for goals in life that we see everything, including being human, as a means to an end.

But there is no reward for being virtuous and human apart from that, in itself, it fulfils our nature."

LEADING BUSINESS ORGANISATIONS WITH INTEGRITY AND EFFECTIVENESS

MANAGING TO BE HUMAN

BRIAN F. SMYTH

END OF DAY

WELL DONE.

HOPE YOU ENJOYED LIVING THE EARTHY AND THE ORDINARY TODAY.

WHAT DISCOVERIES DID YOU MAKE OR WHAT DID YOU MOST ENJOY ABOUT YOUR WORLD AND YOUR LIFE TODAY?

GO TO SLEEP TONIGHT FULL OF TRUST IN THE WORLD AND IN LIFE.

DAY 7

Today is a day where you don't take anything at face value, but are always trying to understand the underlying, hidden truths.

Today you can realize and appreciate that nothing is exactly as it seems and that reality is often hidden behind illusions....or so say numerologists.

And our friend Albert Einstein agrees!

The important thing is not to stop questioning.
Curiosity has its own reasons for existing.

One cannot help but be in awe when he contemplates
the mysteries of eternity, of life, of the marvellous
structure of reality. It is enough if one tries merely to
comprehend a little of this mystery every day.

Never lose a holy curiosity

Albert Einstein

**Today is a day when you can discover that
you are in fact living in a world of miracles.**

67

A stranger arrived to a house in a village looking for something to eat.

"I'm sorry," a woman in the house said, "I have nothing in the house to eat."

"Don't worry," the man said, "I have a soup stone in my satchel and if you give me a big pot of boiling water, I'll make the most delicious soup in the world.

The woman put the pot of water on the fire and told her neighbours about the soup stone and they all gathered around to see the soup.

The stranger dropped the stone into the water and tasted it saying. "Ah delicious! All it needs is some potatoes."

One person said they had potatoes and went and got them.

"Excellent", said the stranger, "if we only had some meat it would be an even tastier stew."

When another neighbour brought some meat he tasted it again, "Wonderful, now a few vegetables."

Several neighbours brought vegetables but also bread, salt and pepper and fruit and other things too.

They all sat down to a delicious meal, their very first common meal.

When they went to look for the stranger to thank him for the soup stone, he had gone.

MIRACLES

IT ISN'T AS IF LIFE IS NOT FULL OF MIRACLES.
IT'S MORE THAN THAT: IT IS MIRACULOUS,
AND ANYONE WHO STOPS
TAKING IT FOR GRANTED
WILL SEE IT AT ONCE.

Just how much of your life and where you are now has been planned by you?

What part has chance, luck, coincidence, fortune, events played in it?

If this was so in the past, why not trust that it will be so in the future and trust it?

Feel good today that you are in good hands.

Work today to realise that you are part of a whole massive enterprise and that you are partnering with the mystery of life in that.

Find two or three little 'miracles' today and when you do, smile.

Smile now. Why not?

TO HELP YOU SEE HOW YOUR WORLD, YOUR DAY IS FULL OF MAGIC, SURPRISES, MYSTERIES AND DEEPER MEANING YOU HAVE SEVERAL PEOPLE WHO WANT TO TELL YOU THEIR STORIES.

PYOTRILYICH TCHAIKOVSKY

DEAN MARTIN

ROBERT BROWNING

TOM JONES

EVA PERON

ANNA KOURNIKOVA

CHRISTY MOORE

GUSTAV MAHLER

PAUL GAUGIN

ALBERT CAMUS

WHO WOULD YOU LIKE TO HELP YOU OPEN YOUR EYES TO WONDER AND SURPRISE TODAY? YOU CAN ONLY PICK A MAXIMUM OF 3.

WHAT QUALITIES DO THEY HAVE THAT YOU WOULD LIKE TO HAVE?
WHAT QUALITIES DO YOU HAVE THAT YOU ARE EITHER NOT SUFFICIENTLY AWARE OF OR ARE NOT PUTTING TO ENOUGH GOOD USE?
HOW CAN YOU PRACTISE AND LIVE THESE TODAY?

WE ARE TOLD THAT WE ASCENDED TO BECOME THE LORDS AND POSSESSORS OF NATURE, DOMESTICATING PLANTS AND ANIMALS, HARNESSING NATURAL FORCES, CONQUERING DISEASES, LAYING BARE THE DEEPEST SECRETS OF THE UNIVERSE.

MAYBE THIS IS NOT RIGHT and we need to move from an attitude of conquerors and colonisers of nature etc.

To one of respectful partners seeking to explore and share our mutual secrets in relationships of care and oneness.

See if you can live out of THIS version, THIS truth today.

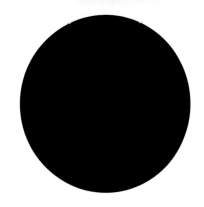
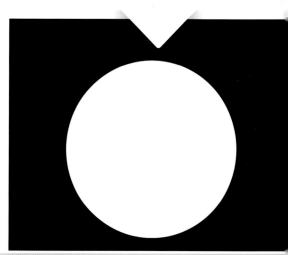

LISTEN TO

MAGICAL MYSTERY TOUR
BY
THE BEATLES

SCAN WITH SMARTPHONE

Joy's Magic

Joy's the magic sweet,
That makes Youth's pulses beat,
Puts music in young feet,
The old heart hears, the sad heart hears, that 's near it:
And Joy's the pleasant pain,
That holds us, heart and brain,
When Old Age, sound and sane,
With memories nears, long memories nears the spirit.

Joy's the witchery rare,
That on the face of Care
Puts smiles; and rapture where
Love holds her breath, her heart's wild breath, to still her:

And Joy it is that plays
On Time's old lute of days
As Life goes on her ways
With thoughts of Death, gray thoughts of Death, that chill her.

Madison Julius Cawein

TODAY

1 LOOK IN A DRAWER OR PRESS OR PLACE YOU HAVE NOT LOOKED IN FOR A WHILE AND FIND SOMETHING INTERESTING.

2 READ A PAGE – ANY PAGE – FROM THE BIBLE (OR THE KORAN, BHAGAVAD GITA, ETC...) AND HEAR WHAT IT IS SAYING TO YOU.

3 WHAT WAS YOUR FAVOURITE FAIRY STORY AS A CHILD?

WHY DO YOU STILL LIKE IT?

SIMBA'S
TIP FOR TODAY

... from his book: *Believe it - It's a Dog's life*

RUN, ROMP
AND PLAY DAILY

YOUR BRAIN
TEASER FOR TODAY

An aged and, it appears, somewhat eccentric king wants to pass his throne on to one of his two sons. He decrees that a horse race shall be held and that the son who owns the slower horse shall become king. The sons, each fearing that the other will cheat by having his horse go less fast than it is capable of, ask a wise man's advice (probably a Maybe advisor!).

With only two words the wise man insures that the race will be fair.

What does he say?

YOUR
MANAGEMENT
MESSAGE
FOR
TODAY
IS

Margaret Wheatley says "I want to surrender my care of the universe and become a participating member in an organisation that moves gracefully with its environment, trusting in the unfolding dance of order."

LEADING BUSINESS ORGANISATIONS
WITH INTEGRITY AND EFFECTIVENESS

MANAGING
TO BE
HUMAN

BRIAN F. SMYTH

END OF DAY

YOU HAVE TO RECALL AT LEAST TWO MIRACLES OR MAJOR DISCOVERIES FROM TODAY.

WERE YOU ABLE TO TRUST THINGS TODAY…THAT THEY WOULD BE OK?

WHAT MYSTERY IS AT WORK IN YOU RIGHT NOW?

"It is an inference from Quantum Theory that events that are separated in space and that are without possibility of connection through interaction are correlated in a way that it can be shown is incapable of a detailed causal explanation."

David Bohm

"What a fine flock of sheep" a stranger said to a farmer, "How much would you say they walk each day?"
"Which ones, the white ones or the black ones?" the farmer answered.
"The white ones", the stranger answered.
"Well, the white ones walk about four miles a day."
"And the black ones?"
"The black ones too."
"And how much grass would you say they eat each day"
"Which ones, the white or the black?"
"The white ones" the stranger answered.
"Well, the white ones eat about four pounds of grass each day."
"And the black ones?"
"The black ones too."
"And how much wool would you say they give each year?"
"Well, I'd say the white ones give some six pounds of wool each."
"And the black ones?"
"The black ones too."
"Mind if I ask you why you keep dividing your sheep into white and black each time?" the stranger asked.
"Well" said the farmer, "that's only natural because the white ones are mine."
"And the black ones?"
"The black ones too" answered the farmer.

IS IT TRUE THAT THERE ARE NO MORE THAN FIVE CONNECTING LINKS BETWEEN YOU AND ANYBODY ELSE IN THE WORLD?

TEST IT!

DO YOU BELIEVE IN THE BUTTERFLY EFFECT? THAT A BUTTERFLY FLAPPING ITS WINGS IN BRAZIL CAN CAUSE A TORNADO IN THE U.S? ROBERT DONAGHY SAYS:

"While the butterfly does not cause the tornado, the flap of its wings is an essential part of the initial conditions resulting in a tornado."

MAKE A CONNECTION WITH SOMEONE NEW TODAY OR WITH SOMEONE WITH WHOM YOU HAVE NOT BEEN IN CONTACT FOR A LONG TIME.

WHAT CONNECTS EVERY ASPECT OR AREA OF YOUR LIFE?

DRAW THIS QUICKLY ON A PAGE.

Do you wish the world were better?
Let me tell you what to do:
Set a watch for your actions,
Keep them always straight and true;
Rid your mind of selfish motives;
Let your thoughts be clean and high.
You can make a little Eden
Of the sphere you occupy.

Do you wish the world were wiser?
Well, suppose you made a start,
By accumulating wisdom
In the scrapbook of your heart:
Do not waste one page on folly;
Live to learn, and learn to live.
If you want to give men knowledge
You must get it, ere you give.

Do you wish the world were happy?
Then remember day by day
Just to scatter seeds of kindness
As you pass along the way;
For the pleasures of the many
May be oft times traced to one,
As the hand that plants an acorn
Shelters armies from the sun.

Ella Wheeler Wilcox

CONNECTIONS - THE MOON AND THE EARTH

One of the few men to walk on the moon tells how he had to suppress his natural, artistic instincts when he got there.

He remembered looking back at Earth and being enraptured by the sight. For a while, he stood rooted to the ground, thinking, "My, that's lovely!"

Then, he quickly shook the mood off and said to himself, "Stop wasting your time and go collect rocks."

SEVERAL PEOPLE WANT TO CONNECT WITH YOU TODAY:

NELSON ROCKEFELLER

DUSTIN HOFFMAN

BILLY ECKSTINE

THE EDGE

ELIZABETH KUBLER-ROSS

CHRIS EUBANK

MARTY FELDMAN

RICHARD I THE LIONHEART

EMPEROR HORIKAWA

SIGOURNEY WEAVER

WITH WHICH 2 OR 3 OF THESE DO YOU FEEL CONNECTED TODAY OR WOULD LIKE TO BE CONNECTED WITH? THERE ARE CONNECTIONS.

WHAT QUALITIES DO THEY HAVE THAT YOU WOULD LIKE TO HAVE?
WHAT QUALITIES DO YOU HAVE THAT YOU ARE EITHER NOT SUFFICIENTLY AWARE OF OR ARE NOT
PUTTING TO ENOUGH GOOD USE?
HOW CAN YOU PRACTISE AND LIVE THESE TODAY?

Be grateful and in awe every time you turn on power or connect to electricity or the internet.

Fix or repair something that has been broken.

Today, see if you can connect two people who have not been in touch.

One day I wrote her name upon the strand,
But came the waves and washed it away:
Again I write it with a second hand,
But came the tide, and made my pains his prey.
Vain man, said she, that doest in vain assay,
A mortal thing so to immortalize,
For I myself shall like to this decay,
And eek my name be wiped out likewise.
Not so, (quod I) let baser things devise
To die in dust, but you shall live by fame:
My verse, your virtues rare shall eternize,
And in the heavens write your glorious name.
Where whenas death shall all the world subdue,
Our love shall live, and later life renew.

Edmund Spenser

No man is an island,
Entire of itself,
Every man is a piece of the continent,
A part of the main.
If a clod be washed away by the sea,
Europe is the less.
As well as if a promontory were.
As well as if a manor of thy friend's
Or of thine own were:
Any man's death diminishes me,
Because I am involved in mankind,
And therefore never send to know
for whom the bell tolls;
It tolls for thee.

John Donne

NEWTON AND MANY OTHERS TELL US THAT ANY PHENOMENON, ALL OF MOVEMENT, ALL OF LIFE, IS THE RESULT OF THE SUM TOTAL OF FORCES ACTING UPON OBJECTS.

HOWEVER there are many who see that that is no longer true and that everything is alive and vibrant, full of life and meaning and purpose and constantly seeking its own fulfilment in the fulfilment of the whole.

Power and energy come from within, from the inside, not the outside.

Can you live out of this internal power today and see this vibrancy and life in everything around you?

LISTEN TO
THE BONES
BY
ALICE IN CHAINS

SCAN WITH SMARTPHONE

YOUR BRAIN TEASER FOR TODAY

You are conducting a census and call to a house and ask the woman in the house how many people live in her house and what their ages are.

The woman tells you her three daughters live in the house, that the product of their ages is thirty-six, and that the sum of their ages is the number of the house next door. You go next door and look at the number of the house but you still can't work it out. The woman then tells you, "My oldest daughter is sleeping upstairs."

And then you get it!
What are the daughters' ages and how did you work it out or know?

YOUR
MANAGEMENT
MESSAGE
FOR
TODAY
IS

You are the centre of a set of relationships. How you are with these people, treat them, talk to them, relate to them and so on will greatly affect how they are, especially if you are a manager of some of them.

In turn, of course, these people are centres of other circles of relationships, and so they too will have great effects on these people, depending on how they are with these people...and so on it goes. We just do not know the extent of the effects we have on people and how powerful these will be.

You have a lot more power than you probably think!

LEADING BUSINESS ORGANISATIONS
WITH INTEGRITY AND EFFECTIVENESS

MANAGING
TO BE
HUMAN

BRIAN F. SMYTH

END OF DAY

THINK A LITTLE OF YOUR DAY AND WHAT HOLDS OR CONNECTS IT ALL TOGETHER.

THINK QUICKLY OF PEOPLE IN YOUR CIRCLE OF RELATIONSHIPS AND HOW IMPORTANT THEY ARE.

REMEMBER THAT IN YOUR DREAMS, ALL THE BARRIERS AND BOUNDARIES AND SEPARATIONS BETWEEN THE DIFFERENT PARTS OF YOUR LIFE WILL ALL DISAPPEAR...AND **ANYTHING CAN HAPPEN!**

WHILE ASLEEP OR AWAKE!

DAY 9

St. Augustine (B. 354 A.D.) commented on the fact that people talked a lot about the miracle of Jesus turning water into wine but no one talked of the miracle that turns grapes into wine.

Today is about change and transformation, that incessant 'miraculous' process of evolution and improvement going on in the world of which we are all a part.

LOOK AROUND YOU TODAY AND NOTE HOW EVERYTHING
IS CHANGING, THAT THERE IS NOTHING THAT IS NOT CHANGING.

CHANGE TWO THINGS YOU DO TODAY – ONE AT WORK AND
ONE IN YOUR HOME LIFE...NO MATTER WHAT THEY
ARE AND HOW YOU FEEL ABOUT THEM.

WHAT ARE SOME GOOD CHANGES YOU HAVE
MADE IN YOURSELF IN THE PAST YEARS?

WHAT DO YOU MOST NEED TO CHANGE IN YOURSELF?
(IF YOU CAN'T THINK OF ANYTHING, ASK A FRIEND!)

WHAT IS ONE MAJOR CHANGE THAT IS NEEDED IN YOUR
WORK AREA THAT IS CRYING OUT TO BE CHANGED?

*There is no intelligence where there
is no change and no need of change*

HG Wells

A great festival was to be held in a village and each villager was asked to contribute by pouring a bottle of wine into a giant barrel.

When the banquet began and the barrel was tapped what came out was water!

One of the villagers had this thought: "If I pour a bottle of water in that giant barrel, no one will notice the difference."

But it hadn't occurred to him that everyone else in the village would have the same thought!

YOU HAVE LOTS OF INTERESTING AND SOME BEAUTIFUL AND WONDERFUL PEOPLE TO HELP YOU TO CHANGE TODAY

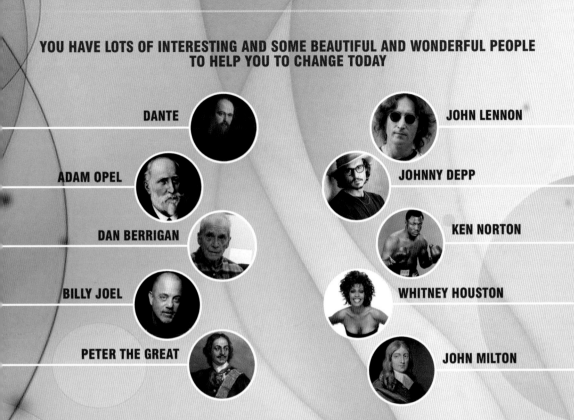

DANTE

JOHN LENNON

ADAM OPEL

JOHNNY DEPP

DAN BERRIGAN

KEN NORTON

BILLY JOEL

WHITNEY HOUSTON

PETER THE GREAT

JOHN MILTON

CHOOSE ONE OR TWO AS YOUR MODELS AND COMPANIONS TO GUIDE AND SUPPORT YOU IN MAKING CHANGES HAPPEN.

WHAT QUALITIES DO THEY HAVE THAT YOU WOULD LIKE TO HAVE?
WHAT QUALITIES DO YOU HAVE THAT YOU ARE EITHER NOT SUFFICIENTLY AWARE OF OR ARE NOT PUTTING TO ENOUGH GOOD USE?
HOW CAN YOU PRACTISE AND LIVE THESE TODAY?

A Secret

A little baby went to sleep
One night in his white bed,
And the moon came by to take a peep
At the little baby head.

A wind, as wandering winds will do,
Brought to the baby there
Sweet smells from some quaint flower that grew
Out on some hill somewhere.

And wind and flower and pale moonbeam
About the baby's bed
Stirred and woke the funniest dream
In the little sleepy head.

He thought he was all sorts of things
From a lion to a cat;
Sometimes he thought he flew on wings,
Or fell and fell, so that

When morning broke he was right glad
But much surprised to see
Himself a soft, pink little lad
Just like he used to be.

I would not give this story fame
If there were room to doubt it,
But when he learned to talk, he came
And told me all about it.

John Charles McNeill

IT SUITS SOME POINTS OF VIEW TO BELIEVE THAT PURLY IMPERSONAL FORCES OF PHYSICS ACT UPON A GENERIC MATERIAL SUBSTRATE OF FUNDAMENTAL PARTICLES, AND THAT PHENOMENA ARE THE RESULT OF MATHEMATICALLY DETERMINED INTERACTIONS.

THERE IS A DIFFERENT VIEW which says that our universe is friendly, intelligent, caring and is working and moving towards its beautiful fulfilment.

Your part in that movement is important.

Your cooperation and contribution is what will give you greatest joy.

Can you find ways to play that part, your part today?

LISTEN TO

CHANGES
BY
DAVID BOWIE

SCAN WITH SMARTPHONE

Miracles

Why, who makes much of a miracle?
As to me I know of nothing else but miracles,
Whether I walk the streets of Manhattan,
Or dart my sight over the roofs of houses toward the sky,
Or wade with naked feet along the beach just in the edge of the water,
Or stand under trees in the woods,
Or talk by day with any one I love, or sleep in the bed at night with any one I love,
Or sit at table at dinner with the rest,
Or look at strangers opposite me riding in the car,
Or watch honey-bees busy around the hive of a summer forenoon,
Or animals feeding in the fields,
Or birds, or the wonderfulness of insects in the air,
Or the wonderfulness of the sundown, or of stars shining so quiet and bright,
Or the exquisite delicate thin curve of the new moon in spring;
These with the rest, one and all, are to me miracles,
The whole referring, yet each distinct and in its place.
To me every hour of the light and dark is a miracle,
Every cubic inch of space is a miracle,
Every square yard of the surface of the earth is spread with the same,
Every foot of the interior swarms with the same.

To me the sea is a continual miracle,
The fishes that swim - the rocks - the motion of the waves - the ships
with men in them,

What stranger miracles are there?

Walt Whitman,

YOUR COLOUR FOR TODAY IS **GREEN**...
AND NOTICE ALL THE MANY DIFFERENT AND
CHANGING VARIATIONS OF GREEN YOU SEE.

DRINK A GLASS OF ORANGE JUICE TODAY AND, AS YOU DO, THINK OF ALL THE CHANGES THAT HAPPENED ON ITS WAY TO YOUR MOUTH.

LISTEN TO A PIECE OF MUSIC AND MARVEL AT THE SENSE YOU CAN MAKE OUT OF DISCRETE NOTES PLACED TOGETHER.

LOOK AT WHERE YOU LIVE AND IMAGINE HOW IT HAS MIRACULOUSLY CHANGED IN THE PAST 50 YEARS AND IMAGINE HOW IT WILL BE IN 50 YEARS TIME.

SIMBA'S
TIP FOR TODAY

... From a *Dog's Life! You must be joking!*

AVOID BITING
WHEN A SIMPLE
GROWL WILL DO

YOUR BRAIN
TEASER FOR TODAY

A FEW FUN BRAIN TEASERS FOR YOU TODAY ...

1. There is three errers in this sentence. Can you find them.

2. Do they have a Fourth of July in France?

3. If a plane crashes in the mountains between Austria and Switzerland, where would the survivors be buried?

4. Two men played checkers.
   They played five games and each won the same number of games. How?

YOUR
MANAGEMENT
MESSAGE
FOR
TODAY
IS

We have to question everything and not take anything for granted. We do this as children and we need to continue to do it in our working environments so that we learn and grow and change and find new and better ways and worlds.

This is a challenge. We can take things for granted. We accept what is and believe that the current way of living and being is the only way. We get comfortable with what we have and with how things are.

But, more dangerously, we cease seeing alternatives because we cease looking for them. We can't imagine any other way of being or doing things or any other state of affairs.

ING BUSINESS ORGANISATIONS
H INTEGRITY AND EFFECTIVENESS

ANAGING
TO BE
HUMAN

RIAN F. SMYTH

END OF DAY

WHAT CHANGES DID YOU MAKE TODAY?

WHAT IS ONE THING THAT YOU NOTICED FROM TODAY THAT YOU SHOULD AND WILL CHANGE?

DO YOU FEEL THAT YOU ARE PART OF A WHOLE UNIVERSE THAT IS CONSTANTLY CHANGING? AND YOUR CHANGE IS AN IMPORTANT PART OF THAT.

DAY 10

None of us is perfect but we can yearn for it and we can admire it when we see it.

Today will be a day where you identify and admire beauty and perfection wherever you see it and where you will enjoy some of the really great things in life and in you. You will also look for areas where you can and should and want to up your standards.

What might these be? Where in your life are you 'settling for' things and not taking yourself with the seriousness you deserve?
And, you will love the imperfections in things and in life too.
Love your own weaknesses and failings too.

Not in the sense of doing nothing about them and resting in mediocrity or unhappiness, but in being kind and tolerant with yourself as you strive for the perfection that you crave.

But you are surrounded by excellence so spot it in even the smallest of things. This keyboard that I am using is so full of magic, power, wisdom that it is hard not to be in awe of it. And there is more!

Enjoy it all.

PERFECTION

"WHAT A PRETTY
BABY YOU
HAVE THERE!"

"THIS IS NOTHING!
YOU SHOULD SEE
HIS PHOTOGRAPHS!"

LOTS OF PEOPLE, LIKE YOU, WHO DID NOT WANT TO SETTLE FOR THE ORDINARY OR MEDIOCRITY.

MARTIN LUTHER

GIUSEPPE VERDI

ARTHUR ASHE

HAROLD PINTER

JIMMY DEAN

PATRICK PEARSE

ARNOLD PALMER

RICHARD BURTON

JOSE FELICIANO

ROD STEWART

SEE WHICH ONE OR TWO YOU WOULD LIKE TO HAVE WITH YOU TODAY ON YOUR MARVELLOUS 10TH.
FIND OUT A BIT MORE ABOUT THEM IF YOU NEED TO.

WHAT QUALITIES DO THEY HAVE THAT YOU WOULD LIKE TO HAVE?
WHAT QUALITIES DO YOU HAVE THAT YOU ARE EITHER NOT SUFFICIENTLY AWARE OF OR ARE NOT PUTTING TO ENOUGH GOOD USE?
HOW CAN YOU PRACTISE AND LIVE THESE TODAY?

Friend, hope for the best while you are alive.
Jump into experience while you are alive!
Think...and think...while you are alive.
What you call 'salvation' belongs to the time before death.

If you don't break your ropes while you're alive, do you
think ghosts will do it after?

The idea that the soul will join with the ecstatic
Just because the body is rotten - that is all fantasy.
What is found now is found then.
If you find nothing now,you will simply end up with
an apartment in the City of Death.

If you make love with the divine now, in the next
life you will have the face of satisfied desire.

So plunge into the truth, find out who the Teacher is,
Believe in the Great Sound!

A mouse was in constant distress because of its fear of cats. A magician
took pity on it and turned it into a cat. But then it became afraid of dogs.
So the magician turned it into a dog.

Then it began to fear panthers. So the magician turned it into a panther,
whereupon it was full of fear of hunters. At this point the magician gave up.

He turned it into a mouse again, saying, "Nothing I do for you is going to
be of any help because you have the heart of a mouse."

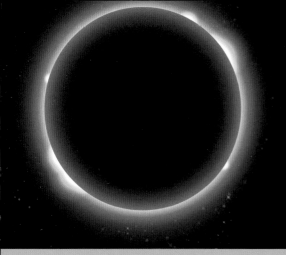

"I never cut my neighbor's throat;
My neighbor's gold I never st[...];
I never spoiled his house and land;
But God have mercy on my soul!

For I am haunted night and day
By all the deeds I have not done;
O unattempted loveliness!
O costly valor never won!

Marguerite Wilkinson

Do two things perfectly today....no matter how simple...
walking, listening to someone, eating.

Eat one thing today with full attention...looking at it beforehand,
examining it, savouring it and then attending to the aftertaste.

Examine a flower today and enjoy its perfection.

A HOLY PERSON, WE WERE TOLD, DOESN'T SUCCUMB TO THE DESIRES OF THE FLESH BUT TAKES THE PATH OF SELF-DENIAL, OF DISCIPLINE, ASCENDING INTO THE REALM OF SPIRIT OR, IN THE SECOND VERSION OF THIS QUEST, INTO THE REALM OF REASON AND THE MIND, PRINCIPLES AND ETHICS.

NO. LIFE IS NOT A BATTLE AGAINST OUR DESIRES.

Quite the contrary.

We need to respect our desires and get in touch with our real and deepest desires.

When we find our true desires and what we really want and need, there will be no need for denying self or disciplining the body. We will have found our heart's desire.

Why not get in touch with your deepest desires today and trust them and live out of them in great joy.

LISTEN TO

HALLELUJAH
BY
LEONARD COHEN

SCAN WITH SMARTPHONE

LOOK FOR THINGS WITH ROUND SHAPES TODAY

THERE ARE LOTS OF THEM

SMILE AND REJOICE WHEN YOU SEE ONE

SIMBA'S
TIP FOR TODAY

IF WHAT YOU WANT
LIES BURIED,
DIG UNTIL YOU FIND IT

YOUR BRAIN
TEASER FOR TODAY

YOU HAVE TWELVE IDENTICAL-LOOKING COINS, ONE OF WHICH IS COUNTERFEIT.

THE COUNTERFEIT COIN IS EITHER HEAVIER OR LIGHTER THAN THE REST.

THE ONLY SCALE AVAILABLE IS A SIMPLE BALANCE.

USING THE BALANCE SCALE ONLY THREE TIMES, FIND THE COUNTERFEIT COIN.

YOUR MANAGEMENT MESSAGE FOR TODAY IS

If it is in our nature to seek perfection and excellence, then why does it not happen as well or as often as we would want or expect it to? Why do we need so much management, training, support and help to achieve higher and better levels of performance if it is in our nature to want to improve anyway? It has to be because something is blocking this natural desire and drive in us. We need to find out what it is.

There are in fact two sets of blocks:

1. How we all block ourselves
2. How we block others and are blocked by others.

If we are going to discover ways of reaching new levels of satisfaction and achievement, then we will need to know and then deal with what is getting in our way, what is preventing us and others from being and doing what we want to be and do.

DING BUSINESS ORGANISATIONS
H INTEGRITY AND EFFECTIVENESS

MANAGING TO BE HUMAN

BRIAN F. SMYTH

END OF DAY

HOPE YOU HAD AN ENJOYABLE DAY AND SAW SOME BEAUTIFUL THINGS.

WHAT IS ONE THING YOU ARE GRATEFUL FOR FROM TODAY EVEN IF THAT IS SOMETHING THAT HAS LITTLE OR NOTHING TO DO WITH YOU DIRECTLY?

WHAT IS ONE THING, BASED ON TODAY, THAT YOU WILL WANT TO WORK ON, DO OR BE BETTER SO YOU ACHIEVE THE EXCELLENCE YOU WERE MADE FOR?

WHAT IS ONE THING THAT CAME CLOSEST TO PERFECTION FOR YOU TODAY – A FLOWER, TREE, MUSIC, SKY, THOUGHT, LANDSCAPE, FOOD, PERSON OR ACTION ETC...?

DAY 11

It was not the words of my enemies that hurt me but the silence of my friends.

Martin Luther King

The family settled down for dinner in a restaurant. The waitress first took the order of the adults, and then asked the seven year old, "What will you have?"

The boy looked around the table timidly and said, "I would like a hotdog."
"No hotdogs", his mother told the waitress. "Get him a steak with potatoes and carrots." The waitress ignored her.

"Do you want ketchup or mustard on your hotdog?" she asked the boy.
"Ketchup" he answered.

"Coming up in a minute" the waitress said.
There was a stunned silence when she left.

Finally the boy looked at everyone and said, "Know what?

She thinks I'm real!"

TODAY IS A DAY FOR FRIENDS AND GETTING CLOSE TO THOSE PEOPLE WHO ARE REALLY A PART OF YOU AND HAVE PLAYED OR DO PLAY A BIG PART IN MAKING OR HELPING YOU TO BE THE PERSON YOU ARE. IT IS ALSO ABOUT LISTENING.

LISTENING

REALLY LISTENING TO PEOPLE,
BUT ALSO LISTENING TO ALL
KINDS OF SOUNDS WITHOUT
INTERPRETING OR ANALYSING THEM.

JUST LISTEN

Today be grateful for your close friends, your dear brother or sister and, if you can, let them know that you appreciate them.

Everyone you are with today, pay attention to THEM.

Watch yourself today drifting back to yourself in conversations and telling YOUR story, YOUR experience, YOUR idea. Stay with the other person.

SOLVING PEOPLES PROBLEMS

The chief executive of a large company was greatly admired for his energy and drive.

But he suffered from one embarrassing weakness: each time he entered the president's office to make his weekly report, he would wet his pants!

The kindly president advised him to see a proctologist. When he appeared before the president the following week his pants were still wet! "Didn't you coo tho prootologiot?" Asked the president.

"No. He was out. I saw a psychologist instead. I'm cured. I no longer feel embarrassed!"

YOU CAN CHOOSE FROM MANY GOOD FRIENDS TO HELP YOU HAVE
A GREAT DAY OF WARMTH AND FRIENDSHIP AND OPENNESS

THOMAS EDISON

SALVADOR DALI

EVA GABOR

PHIL SILVERS

SERGIO MENDES

RICHARD FEYNMAN

JESSE JACKSON

JEREMY PAXMAN

IRVING BERLIN

THOMAS EDISON

SO, WHICH TWO OR THREE WOULD YOU LIKE TO GET TO KNOW BETTER AND TO
ACCOMPANY YOU ON THIS DAY 11?

WHAT QUALITIES DO THEY HAVE THAT YOU WOULD LIKE TO HAVE?
WHAT QUALITIES DO YOU HAVE THAT YOU ARE EITHER NOT SUFFICIENTLY AWARE OF OR ARE NOT
PUTTING TO ENOUGH GOOD USE?
HOW CAN YOU PRACTISE AND LIVE THESE TODAY?

IT IS EASY TO BELIEVE THAT YOU ARE A SOUL ENCASED IN FLESH, SEPARATE FROM THE WORLD AND SEPARATE FROM OTHER SOULS.

BUT IT IS NOT SO.

Separateness is an illusion.

Oneness is the reality. You are as much one with everything else as the leaf is part of the tree and the tree part of its environment.

Why not spot this oneness throughout the day and live out of it.

If you do, you will never feel alone or weak.

LISTEN TO

AMIGO
BY
ROBERTO CARLOS

SCAN WITH SMARTPHONE

SCAN WITH SMARTPHONE

Look for pairs of things and people today.

Eat a pear at some point during the day.

At some point in the day, spend a whole 5 minutes just listening.

FRIEND
Translation of song 'Amigo'

You are my soul brother,
really that brother who on every journey and
every day is always with me.
Even though you are a man you still have the soul
of a child.
The one who gives me his friendship, his respect
and his affection. I remember that together we went
through very difficult moments and you never changed
no matter how strong the winds were. Your heart is a
house with open doors. You really are the most certain
of people at uncertain times.
In certain difficult moments in life we look for somebody
who will help us to find the way out and those words of strength
that have given me hope you give me the certainty that
you are always at my side.
You are my soul friend every day a smile, a warm
hug on every arrival.
You tell me great truths with clear words.
You really are the more secure in insecure times.
I don't need to tell you all this but I do tell you
but it's really good to feel that
you are my great friend.

Observe people today and how they relate to each other and influence each other.

Find out from someone close to you how they or other people see you. Don't be afraid to do this.

Others see how you are and probably talk about how they see you among themselves.

With a stranger or someone you don't know at all, be as personal and attentive as you can with them.

We will meet again my friend,
A hundred years from today
Far away from where we lived
And where we used to play.

We will know each other's eyes
And wonder where we met
Your laugh will sound familiar.
Your heart, I won't forget.

We will meet,
I'm sure of this,
But let's not wait till then...
Let's take a walk beneath the stars
And share this world again.

Ron Atchison

SIMBA'S
TIP FOR TODAY

... from his book: *Enjoy a Dog's Life*

ON WARM DAYS, STOP TO LIE ON YOUR BACK ON THE GRASS

YOUR BRAIN
TEASER FOR TODAY

A customer gives a 20 Euro note to a shop assistant for a book priced at 12 Euro.

Because the shopkeeper was short of change, she changes the €20 at a store next door. She then gives the book and eight euro to the customer. Later the neighbouring storekeeper discovering the €20 note to be counterfeit, returns it to the shopkeeper, who exchanges it for a genuine €20 note.

If the shopkeeper had 100% markup on the book, how much did she actually lose in the transaction?

YOUR
MANAGEMENT
MESSAGE
FOR
TODAY
IS

More and more we are understanding that what matters is not so much our genes but how we respond to our environment.

Our life is not determined by our genes but by our responses to the environmental signals that propel life.

And we are constantly changing and establishing that environment. We can transform an environment by how we are and equally transform a person.

As Goethe said: 'Treat people as they are, and they will remain as they are. Treat people as they can and should be, and they will become as they can and should be.'

DING BUSINESS ORGANISATIONS
TH INTEGRITY AND EFFECTIVENESS

ANAGING
TO BE
HUMAN

BRIAN F. SMYTH

WHAT IS SOMETHING NEW YOU LEARNED ABOUT SOMEBODY ELSE TODAY?

IS THERE ANYTHING YOU LEARNED ABOUT YOURSELF?

TO WHOM WERE YOU A GOOD FRIEND TODAY?

SAY THANKS TO SOME OF YOUR DEAREST FRIENDS IN YOUR HEART TONIGHT.

DAY 12

To see a World in a Grain of Sand And a Heaven in a Wild Flower
Hold Infinity in the palm of your hand And Eternity in an hour.

William Blake

01 Today is a day of wonder, wonder about the amazing things that can happen and that are happening every day and happening to you and in your world.

02 Look back today at all the surprises in your life to date and the impact of these on the shape your life has taken. Were these all chance?
And, if they were, is not this chance a wonder-full thing.

03 Find examples today of all the wonder in life and all the workings that are going on around us and of which we are a part.

04 Make the 12th a day of wonder and of hope, no matter what is happening or happens.
It is still at work.

I wanted a miracle to convince me.

But here it is, the only possible existing miracle, surrounding me on all sides, and I did not even observe it.

What greater miracles can there be?

Leo Tolstoy

BUT YOU WILL HAVE SOME OTHER WONDERFUL PEOPLE WITH YOU TODAY AS YOU LOOK FOR, ENJOY AND CELEBRATE THE WONDERS OF LIFE AND WONDERFUL LIFE.

ABRAHAM LINCOLN

LIZA MINNELLI

CHARLES DARWIN

CHARLES DUMAS

FRANCO ZEFFIRELLI

TONY HANCOCK

HOMER SIMPSON

FLORENCE NIGHTINGALE

JACK KEROUAC

BURT BACHARACH

NOTHING BORING ABOUT THESE PEOPLE. YOU CAN HAVE ONE TO THREE OF THEM WITH YOU TODAY TO HELP YOU SEE AND APPRECIATE THE WONDERS OF LIFE AS WELL AS YOUR OWN WONDERFUL LIFE.

WHAT QUALITIES DO THEY HAVE THAT YOU WOULD LIKE TO HAVE?
WHAT QUALITIES DO YOU HAVE THAT YOU ARE EITHER NOT SUFFICIENTLY AWARE OF OR ARE NOT PUTTING TO ENOUGH GOOD USE?
HOW CAN YOU PRACTISE AND LIVE THESE TODAY?

▷ ▷ ▷ ▷ ▷ ▷ ▷ ▷ ▷ ▷ ▷

Sense of Wonder

When we are born we are full of wonder.
When we grow we start to discover.
When we are told we begin to forget.
When we are old we start to lament.

Wonder is a valuable thing.
It helps us to dance, play and sing.
It makes us remember why we breathe.
It helps us all want to achieve.

Why is it then that we forget?
What wonder does, gives, provokes and lets,
Let us remember the things that we should recall.
The sights, sounds and smells of the wondrous all.

So discover the world,
ourselves and others.
Discover the passion to live,
fight and wonder.

OR

The Thinker

My wife's new pink slippers
have gay pom-poms.
There is not a spot or a stain
on their satin toes or their sides.
All night they lie together
under her bed's edge.
Shivering I catch sight of them
and smile, in the morning.
Later I watch them
descending the stair,
hurrying through the doors
and round the table,
moving stiffly
with a shake of their gay pom-poms!
And I talk to them
in my secret mind
out of pure happiness.

William Carlos Williams

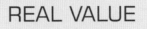

REAL VALUE

A WOMAN TOURIST FROM THE WEST WAS ADMIRING A NATIVE'S NECKLACE. "WHAT IS IT MADE OF?" SHE ASKED.

"ALLIGATOR TEETH, MAM" SAID THE NATIVE.

"OH, I SEE. I WONDER IF THEY HAVE THE SAME VALUE FOR YOU PEOPLE THAT PEARLS HAVE FOR US?"

"NOT QUITE MAM. ANYONE CAN OPEN AN OYSTER."

CAN YOU NAME THE SEVEN WONDERS OF THE WORLD? WHAT ARE SEVEN WONDERS IN YOUR WORLD, YOUR LIFE? FIND THEM. THEY ARE THERE.

LOOK AROUND YOU RIGHT NOW AND DURING THE DAY AND WONDER ABOUT HOW THINGS CAME TO BE AS THEY ARE AND ABOUT THE PEOPLE WHO MADE THEM SO. AREN'T THEY WONDERFUL?

DO YOU WONDER 'WHO WROTE THE BOOK OF LOVE?'. WHAT WOULD BE IN YOUR BOOK OF LOVE?

WHAT DO YOU THINK 'THE THREE THINGS A VISITOR FROM ANOTHER PLANET WOULD WONDER ABOUT IF THEY CAME TO VISIT? AREN'T THEY WORTH WONDERING ABOUT? DOING SOMETHING ABOUT?

Look for light and bright things today and lift your head –and your heart – when you spot them.

What if you slept?
And what if in your sleep, you dreamed?
And what if in your dream,
you went to heaven and there plucked a
strange and beautiful flower?
And what if, when you woke, you had the flower in your hand?
Ah! What then?

Samuel Taylor Coleridge

The Arrow and the Song

I shot an arrow into the air,
It fell to earth, I knew not where;
For, so swiftly it flew, the sight
Could not follow it in its flight.

I breathed a song into the air,
It fell to earth, I knew not where;
For who has sight so keen and strong,
That it can follow the flight of song?

Long, long afterward, in an oak
I found the arrow, still unbroke;
And the song, from beginning to end,
I found again in the heart of a friend.

Henry Longfellow

YOU MAY HAVE HEARD OR READ THAT YOU ARE A CARTESIAN MOTE OF CONSCIOUSNESS LOOKING OUT THROUGH THE EYES OF THE FLESH ROBOT, PROGRAMMED BY ITS GENES TO MAXIMISE REPRODUCTIVE SELF-INTEREST.

MAYBE you also heard a different story.

That you are part of an overall, embracing consciousness that is working through you, with you and that is making available an enormous intelligence that you can be in touch with and use as you need and want.

Why not act out of this story today and everyday. It is a far better and more accurate story.

LISTEN TO

IT´S A WONDERFUL LIFE
BY
BLACK

SCAN WITH SMARTPHONE

SIMBA'S
TIP FOR TODAY

... from his blockbuster book *I'll Give you a Dog's Life*

DELIGHT IN THE SIMPLE JOY OF A LONG WALK

YOUR BRAIN TEASER FOR TODAY

A wine merchant who has asked you to be the executor of his will, dies, leaving his three sons seven barrels full of wine, seven barrels half full of wine, and seven empty barrels.

In his will he specifies that each son shall receive the same number of full, half full and empty barrels.

Can you, as executor, carry out his wish? If so, how?

YOUR
MANAGEMENT
MESSAGE
FOR
TODAY
IS

A failure or refusal to identify a need for things to be different and the lack of belief that they can be so are the single biggest blocks to creativity.

But there always is a need if we want to look for it and we should find it before it finds us.

And so the big sin or temptation is to settle for what we have, simply because it is what we have. We settle for what we have because of the risk of failing if we go after more or better and because it is easier to continue where we are.

DING BUSINESS ORGANISATIONS
H INTEGRITY AND EFFECTIVENESS

MANAGING
TO BE
HUMAN

RIAN F. SMYTH

END OF DAY

WHAT SEVEN WONDERS OF YOUR WORLD DID YOU FIND TODAY?

WHAT IS ONE THING TODAY THAT GAVE YOU MORE HOPE IN LIFE AND IN THE FUTURE?

WHAT IS ONE THING YOU DID TODAY THAT HOPEFULLY GAVE SOMEONE MORE HOPE...IN PEOPLE, IN LIFE, IN THEMSELVES?

WHY ARE YOU WONDERFUL TOO?

DAY 13

The only good luck many great men ever had was being born with the ability and determination to overcome bad luck.

Channing Pollock

> Between stimulus and response, there is a space. In that space is our power to choose our response. In our response lies our growth and our freedom.
>
> ## Viktor Frankl

You may be in great form today and everything going really well and yet it is a day where you will practise being ready for and befriending upsets, disappointments, 'down' moments. If it is NOT a wonderful day, then it will be an even better chance to live through emptiness, bleakness, nothingness.
Think you can do that? It will be great anyway.

In case you think this means that you need to be sad or unhappy, the opposite is the case. Today will be about your faith in your own spirit to be able to live through tough and dark times.

Be ready for upsets today and smile when you hear of them or come across them.

Think of one or two things in your life that, at the time, seemed really bad news but which turned out ok or turned into something really good.

Life knows what is good for us better than we do.

A group of tourists stranded in countryside were given old food to eat. Before eating it they decided to test it by giving some of it to a dog who seemed to enjoy it and suffered no after effects.

The following day, they learned that the dog had died.

Everyone became panic-stricken and many began to vomit and complained of fever and dysentery. They called a doctor to treat the victims for food poisoning.

The doctor began by asking what happened to the body of the dog so he could establish the kind of poisoning.

Enquiries were made.

Eventually a local came forward and said: "I threw it in a ditch after I found it run over by a car."

TO HELP YOU THROUGH DIFFICULT TIMES, TODAY OR SOME OTHER DAY, YOU HAVE SOME REALLY STRONG AND GOOD PEOPLE WITH YOU.

NAPOLEON BONAPARTE

GUY FAWKES

OLIVER REED

THOMAS JEFFERSON

RAINER WERNER FASSBINDER

BUTCH CASSIDY

SEAMUS HEANEY

SAMUEL BECKETT

JOE BUGNER

JULIUS NYERERE

WHAT STRONG COMPANIONS YOU HAVE HERE – PEOPLE WHO KNEW BOTH THE DARK AND THE BRIGHT SIDE. CHOOSE ONE OR TWO TO BE WITH YOU THIS DAY, THIS MONTH.

WHAT QUALITIES DO THEY HAVE THAT YOU WOULD LIKE TO HAVE? WHAT QUALITIES DO YOU HAVE THAT YOU ARE EITHER NOT SUFFICIENTLY AWARE OF OR ARE NOT PUTTING TO ENOUGH GOOD USE? HOW CAN YOU PRACTISE AND LIVE THESE TODAY?

Awake and Alert today!

BE READY FOR SURPRISES OR UPSETS TODAY... OR DISAPPOINTMENTS.

WHEN THINGS GO WRONG TODAY, ACCEPT THEM AND MOVE ON. YOU CAN!

STAY WITH ANY MOMENTS OR FEELINGS OF SADNESS OR LOWNESS AND WORK FROM THEM. YOU CAN! DON'T RUN FROM THEM.

BE ABLE WITH KIPLING TO MEET WITH TRIUMPH AND DISASTER AND TREAT THOSE TWO IMPOSTORS JUST THE SAME?

I am contradiction.
I am afraid of commitment, and rejection, and honesty, and love.
I am afraid of feeling too much.
I am afraid of feeling nothing.
I am sometimes ecstatically happy and dance and sing and shout to the world.
I am sometimes so wrecked by sadness I can't catch my breath.
I often have the overwhelming urge to scream.
I often have the overwhelming urge for a steady, strong, embrace.
I am not who I was yesterday.
I am not who I will be tomorrow.

the yes and no of emptiness.

I am longing. I am waiting.
I am want.
I am an empty vessel, a blank page, a beating heart.
I am a mad woman.
I am a child of God.
I am the yes. I am the no.

Melinda

131

SOME REDUCTIONIST SCIENTISTS TELL US THAT THOUGHT IS AN ELECTROCHEMICAL IMPULSE; LOVE A HORMONAL CASCADE THAT REWIRES OUR BRAINS.

YES, EVERYTHING IS REDUCIBLE to ever less meaningful levels but, it is thought and love that hold the real meaning of everything and bring all together.

A kiss can be a chemical encounter of cells…or much more.

Living happens at the higher and richer level.

See if you can find this higher level in everything you do today. It IS there to be found.

LISTEN TO

ANTHEM
BY
LEONARD COHEN

SCAN WITH SMARTPHONE

Cancer is so limited ...

It cannot cripple love.
It cannot shatter hope.
It cannot corrode faith.
It cannot eat away peace.
It cannot destroy confidence.
It cannot kill friendship.
It cannot cut out memories.
It cannot silence courage.
It cannot invade the soul.
It cannot reduce eternal life.
It cannot quench the spirit.
It cannot lessen the power of
the resurrection

I walked a mile with pleasure;
She chatted all the way.
But left me none the wiser
For all she had to say.

I walked a mile with sorrow
And ne'er a word said she
But all the things I learned from her
When Sorrow walked with me!

Robert Browning

As You Go Through Life

Don't look for the flaws as you go through life;
And even when you find them,
It is wise and kind to be somewhat blind,
And look for the virtue behind them;
For the cloudiest night has a hint of light
Somewhere in its shadows hiding;
It's better by far to hunt for a star,
Than the spots on the sun abiding.

The current of life runs ever away
To the bosom of God's great ocean.
Don't set your force 'gainst the river's course,
And think to alter its motion.

Don't waste a curse on the universe,
Remember, it lived before you;
Don't butt at the storm with your puny form,
But bend and let it go o'er you.

The world will never adjust itself
To suit your whims to the letter,
Some things must go wrong your whole life long,
And the sooner you know it the better.
It is folly to fight with the Infinite,
And go under at last in the wrestle.
The wiser man shapes into God's plan,
As water shapes into a vessel.

Ella Wheeler Wilcox

SIMBA'S
TIP FOR TODAY

... from his work: *Come and Enjoy a Dog's Life with Me*

WHEN SOMEONE OR LIFE GIVES YOU A KICK, TRUST YOU WILL GET OVER IT

YOUR BRAIN
TEASER FOR TODAY

You have three strange friends, Jim, Mark and Sally who have unusual pets.
Jim calls his Jarvis, Mark calls his Marvin and Sally calls hers Spot.
One of the pets is a baboon, another is a penguin, and the third is the largest rabbit in the world.

You have to tell us the name of the largest rabbit in the world.

Some more information for you:

1. The rabbit played soccer with his owner yesterday.
2. Jim's leg has been in a cast for 2 months.
3. The baboon's owner goes horseback riding every Saturday with one of the other pet lovers.
4. The baboon bit Marvin.

Ok? So, what is the name of the largest rabbit in the world?

YOUR MANAGEMENT MESSAGE FOR TODAY IS

Our big allies in making the most of every day and of our lives are problems and surprises.

These are messages for us to see what actually is and they attempt to rid us of our sleepy state of not seeing what is really going on.

To hear the message that surprises us and to face up to problems, we have to do two things:

a. See and feel what is going on and to do so in an incredibly honest and courageous way.

b. Open our mind to and explore all the possibilities the situation offers us.

LEADING BUSINESS ORGANISATIONS
WITH INTEGRITY AND EFFECTIVENESS

MANAGING
TO BE
HUMAN

BRIAN F SMYTH

END OF DAY

CELEBRATE ALL THE OCCASIONS DURING THE DAY WHEN YOU ENCOUNTERED DIFFICULT MOMENTS WHETHER THESE WERE REAL OR JUST IN YOUR OWN HEAD.

FORGIVE YOURSELF IF YOU DID NOT HANDLE EVERYTHING AS WELL AS YOU WOULD HAVE LIKED OR BECAME IMPATIENT, IRRITABLE, UPSET ETC.

BE GRATEFUL FOR WHAT YOU HAVE AND PUT YOUR TRUST IN LIFE OF WHICH YOU ARE JUST ONE MORE PART, IMPORTANT AS THAT PART IS.

IF THERE WAS SOME SITUATION THAT YOU FEEL YOU DID NOT HANDLE AS WELL AS YOU LIKED TODAY, REPLAY IT NOW IN YOUR HEAD, HANDLING IT AS YOU WOULD HAVE LIKED TO HAVE HANDLED IT AND IN LINE WITH THE BEAUTIFUL PERSON YOU REALLY ARE.

DAY 14

This is your one and only precious life.
Somebody's going to decide how it's going to be
lived and that person had better be you.

Harry Casey

TODAY'S THEME IS ABOUT THE STAGES IN LIFE THAT WE PASS THROUGH.

CAN YOU IDENTIFY THE VARIOUS STAGES IN YOUR LIFE AND WHERE THIS ONE COMES?

IT IS IMPORTANT TO BE AWARE OF THESE STAGES AND HANDLE THEM WELL.

IT IS ALSO IMPORTANT TO MOVE FROM ONE STAGE TO THE NEXT AT AN APPROPRIATE TIME AND NOT STAY TOO LONG IN ANY ONE STAGE.

WHAT DOES THIS STAGE IN YOUR LIFE CALL FOR FROM YOU? HOW WELL ARE YOU HANDLING IT?

BE AWARE OF THIS AS YOU GO THROUGH THE DAY.

MAKING THE MOST OF EVERY STAGE IN LIFE

There was a crowd in the doctor's waiting room: an elderly gentleman rose and approached the receptionist.

"Madam," he said courteously, "My appointment was for 10 o'clock and it's almost 11 now. I cannot wait any longer. Would you kindly give me an appointment for another day?"

One woman in the crowd leaned over to another and said, "He must be at least 80 years old. What sort of urgent business can he have that he cannot afford to wait?"

The man overheard the whispered remark. He turned to the lady, bowed and said, "I'm 87 years old, lady.

Which is precisely the reason why I cannot afford to waste a single minute of the precious time I have left."

Let My Life Sing

Make me too brave to lie or be unkind
Make me too understanding, too, to mind
The little hurts companions give, and friends,
The careless hurts that no one quite intends.
May I forget
What ought to be forgotten, and recall,
Unfailing, all
That ought to be recalled, each kindly thing,
Forgetting what might sting.
To all upon my way,
Day after day,
Let me be joy, be hope!
Let my life sing.

LOOK AROUND
YOU TODAY
AT PEOPLE
YOU KNOW
AND SEE
WHAT STAGE OF
LIFE YOU THINK
THEY ARE AT

THINK OF WHAT
A NEW STAGE
WOULD
BE AND LOOK LIKE IF
YOU DECIDED
TO MOVE TO ONE

TURN SOME PAGE
TODAY – BE IT IN A
BOOK, SOMETHING
YOU HAVE BEEN
HOLDING ON TO,
OR SOMETHING YOU
NEED TO COMPLETE

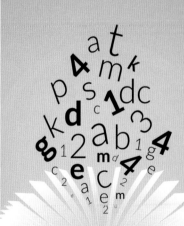

THE ONLY PURPOSE OF LIFE, WE HAVE BEEN TOLD, IS SIMPLY TO LIVE, TO SURVIVE AND REPRODUCE, TO MAXIMISE RATIONAL SELF-INTEREST.

MAYBE THIS IS NOT SO AT ALL.

Maybe Life belongs to the whole and every life joyfully contributes to the beauty and fulfilment of the whole and so shares and partakes in that wonderful fulfilment.

Maybe that is a far better —and more authentic — way to see things... and to live... today... and every day.

LISTEN TO

LIFE
BY
DES´REE

SCAN WITH SMARTPHONE

Yesterday is but a dream,
tomorrow a vision,
but today well lived,
makes every yesterday
a dream of happiness;
and every tomorrow
a vision of hope.
Look well, therefore,
to this day.

SIMBA'S
TIP FOR TODAY

BE LOYAL,
NO MATTER
WHAT OTHERS DO
YOU'RE YOU

YOUR BRAIN
TEASER FOR TODAY

Three intelligent men, applying for a job, seem equal in all pertinent attributes, so the prospective employer, also an intelligent man, sets a simple problem for them. The job, he says, will go to the first applicant to solve it.

A mark is placed on each man's forehead. The three are told that each has either a black mark or a white mark, and each is to raise his hand if he sees a black mark on the forehead of either of the other two.

The first one to tell of what colour he has and how he arrived at his answer will get the job. Each man raised his hand, and after a few seconds one man comes up with the answer.

What colour was his mark and how did he figure it out?

YOUR
MANAGEMENT
MESSAGE
FOR
TODAY
IS

We have to question everything and not take anything for granted. We do this as children and we need to continue to do it in our working environments so that we learn and grow and change and find new and better ways and worlds. This is a challenge. We can take things for granted. We accept what is and believe that the current way of living and being is the only way.

We get comfortable with what we have and with how things are. But, more dangerously, we cease seeing alternatives because we cease looking for them. We can't imagine any other way of being or doing things or any other state of affairs.

DING BUSINESS ORGANISATIONS
TH INTEGRITY AND EFFECTIVENESS

MANAGING
TO BE
HUMAN

BRIAN F. SMYTH

END OF DAY

IT'S THE END OF THE DAY. IS THERE ANYTHING THAT YOU THOUGHT OF TODAY

THAT YOU NEED TO END IN ORDER TO BEGIN SOMETHING NEW?

WHAT IS ONE CHANGE THAT YOU HANDLED WELL IN YOUR LIFE?

WERE THERE ANY CHALLENGES OR INVITATIONS, OR EVEN HINTS, TODAY THAT
YOU MIGHT CHANGE SOMETHING.

DAY 15

Most people are so afraid to die that, from their efforts to avoid death, they never live.

Anthony de Mello

TODAY IS ABOUT BEING YOUNG AND FEELING YOUNG AND ENJOYING THE YOUNG.

YOU WILL FEEL YOUNG, NO MATTER WHAT AGE YOU ARE AND WILL DO SOME YOUNG THINGS.

YOU WILL RECALL HOW YOU WERE WHEN YOU WERE YOUNG AND WILL ALSO RECALL THE HOPES AND ASPIRATIONS AND DREAMS YOU HAD WHEN YOU WERE YOUNG(ER).

TODAY YOU WILL GET IN TOUCH WITH THE 'YOUNG' IN YOU.

YOU WILL ACT YOUNG – FRESH, SEEING THINGS ANEW, DOING SOME NEW THINGS.

YOU WILL HAVE A GREAT DAY 15 AND BE REFRESHED AND RENEWED.

THE NAKED TRUTH THROUGH THE EYES OF LITTLE ONES

Tommy just got back from the beach.

"Were there other children there?" Asked his mother.
"Yes," said Tommy.

"Boys or girls?"

"How could I know! They didn't have any clothes on."

Two women friends met after many years.

"What happened to your son?" one woman asked.

"My son? The poor, poor lad," the other woman answered.

"He got married to a girl, who won't do a stitch of work in the house. She won't cook, she won't clean, she won't iron. The poor boy even has to bring her breakfast in bed."

"That's awful!" her friend replied.

"And what about your daughter?"

"Oh! She's the lucky one.
She married an angel.

He won't let her do a thing in the house and does the cooking, and cleaning and ironing. She even gets her breakfast in bed every morning."

TO HELP YOU BE YOUNG TODAY YOU HAVE SOME WONDERFUL 'YOUNG' PEOPLE ALONGSIDE YOU, ENCOURAGING YOU, SUPPORTING YOU AND EVEN ATTACKING YOU FOR ACTING OLD.

REMBRANDT

AGATHA CHRISTIE

EDWARD SHACKLETON

JOHN KENNETH GALBRAITH

JACQUES DERRIDA

TOMMY LEE JONES

WALTER SCOTT

MARCO POLO

OSCAR ROMERO

OSCAR PETERSON

WHICH TWO WILL YOU CHOOSE TO HELP YOU ENJOY BEING YOUNG TODAY?
WHAT DO YOU MOST LIKE ABOUT THEIR 'YOUTHFULNESS'?

WHAT QUALITIES DO THEY HAVE THAT YOU WOULD LIKE TO HAVE?
WHAT QUALITIES DO YOU HAVE THAT YOU ARE EITHER NOT SUFFICIENTLY AWARE OF OR ARE NOT PUTTING TO ENOUGH GOOD USE?
HOW CAN YOU PRACTISE AND LIVE THESE TODAY?

WHAT DID YOU MOST LIKE ABOUT BEING YOUNG?

LOOK AT YOUNG PEOPLE TODAY AND SEE WHAT YOU SEE.

DO SOMETHING TODAY THAT YOU DID WHEN YOUNGER OR THAT YOUNGER PEOPLE DO.

DECIDE TO DO ONE THING THAT WILL KEEP YOU YOUNG NO MATTER HOW DELIGHTFULLY OLD YOU MAY BE.

TALK TO...OR RATHER LISTEN TO A YOUNG PERSON TODAY...REALLY LISTEN.... AND LEARN.

IT HAS BEEN SAID THAT YOU ARE JUST A MASS, A CONGLOMERATION OF PARTICLES OPERATING ACCORDING TO THE IMPERSONAL FORCES OF PHYSICS.

BUT MAYBE IT IS NOT SO AT ALL.

Maybe you are part of a beautiful intelligence that is at work in and through you and everything else.

Maybe you make your own unique contribution to that wonderful intelligence and process.

Your contribution is an important part of that greater intelligence and power.

Can you find ways to make that contribution today in what you do or to see how you are already making that rich contribution so you can celebrate it?

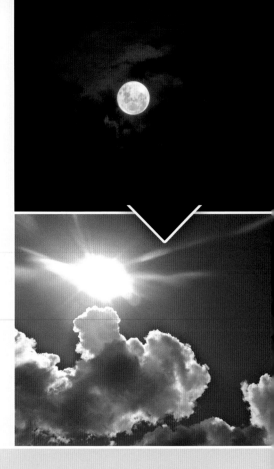

LISTEN TO
FOREVER YOUNG
BY
BOB DYLAN

SCAN WITH SMARTPHONE

Beyond our ideas of right-doing and
wrong-doing,
there is a field. I'll meet you there.
When the soul lies down in that grass,
the world is too full to talk about.
Ideas, language, even the phrase 'each other'
doesn't make sense any more.

Rumi

When I see the young men play,
Young methinks I am as they;
And my aged thoughts laid by,
To the dance with joy I fly:
Come, a flowery chaplet lend me;
Youth and mirthful thoughts attend me:
Age be gone, we'll dance among
Those that young are, and be young:
Bring some wine, boy, fill about;
You shall see the old man's stout;
Who can laugh and tipple too,
And be mad as well as you.

Anacreon

SIMBA'S
TIP FOR TODAY

WHEN YOU'RE HAPPY, DANCE AROUND AND WAG YOUR ENTIRE BODY

YOUR BRAIN TEASER FOR TODAY

Your brain teaser for today to keep your mind fresh and young:

Supply a digit for each letter so that the equation is correct.

A given letter always represents the same digit

$$
\begin{array}{r}
A\ B\ C\ D\ E \\
\times\ 4 \\
\hline
E\ D\ C\ B\ A
\end{array}
$$

Parents:

"Why is it that though Johnny is younger than you, his marks at school are always better?"

Seven year old:

"I don't know! Could it be that it's because Johnny's parents are cleverer than mine?"

YOUR MANAGEMENT MESSAGE FOR TODAY IS

Creativity needs freedom – freedom from the mind, freedom from knowledge, freedom from prejudices. A creative person is one who can try the new. Like children who are free to love and explore everything new.

'Daddy, is that white, wet noise?' the young kid asks his dad walking along the beach.

'No, son', the father says, 'that's the sea!' As we grow older we learn to adjust to the world around us and, while this is very important, it also builds walls and barriers of fear around us. We daren't appear foolish. As a result, we lose our freedom to think and explore.

LEADING BUSINESS ORGANISATIONS WITH INTEGRITY AND EFFECTIVENESS

MANAGING TO BE HUMAN

BRIAN E. SMYTH

END OF DAY

HOPE YOU ARE NICE AND TIRED LIKE CHILDREN ARE AT THE END OF DAY
WHERE THEY EXTRACTED EVERY BIT OF FUN FROM THEIR DAY.

HOPE, LIKE CHILDREN, YOU ARE LOOKING FORWARD TO ANOTHER
WONDERFUL DAY OF ADVENTURE TOMORROW.

SMILE AT SOMETHING STUPID OR SILLY OR 'IRRESPONSIBLE' YOU DID TODAY.

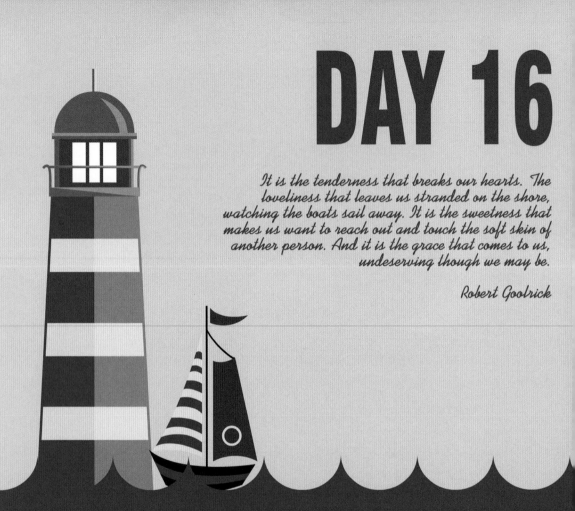

DAY 16

It is the tenderness that breaks our hearts. The loveliness that leaves us stranded on the shore, watching the boats sail away. It is the sweetness that makes us want to reach out and touch the soft skin of another person. And it is the grace that comes to us, undeserving though we may be.

Robert Goolrick

YOUR COLOUR TODAY IS LOVELY PURPLE

TODAY WILL BE A SWEET DAY...WHATEVER IS HAPPENING IN YOUR WORLD OR HAPPENS IN THE COURSE OF THE DAY.

YOU CAN FIND SWEETNESS IN EVERYTHING, EVEN IN SADNESS.

ENJOY ANY SWEET THINGS YOU TASTE TODAY AND TRY TO SAVOUR AT LEAST ONE SWEET THING.

ENJOY OTHER SWEETNESSES TOO.... MUSIC, SOUND OF A BIRD OR THE WIND, THE SWEETNESS OF GETTING SOMETHING JUST RIGHT, THE SWEETNESS OF A HANDSHAKE OR, BETTER STILL, A KISS.

FIND AS MANY SWEET THINGS IN LIFE AND, ESPECIALLY, YOUR OWN DEEP SWEETNESS AS A PERSON AND HUMAN BEING.

SOME SWEET FRIENDS FOR YOU WHO WERE BORN ON THIS DAY

JOSHUA REYNOLDS

EYDIE GORME

GINGER ROGERS

DAVID COPPERFIELD

MARGARET SMITH COURT

MADONNA

MICHAEL FLATLEY

OSCAR WILDE

JOHN BOSCO

JANE AUSTEN

SO, WHICH TWO OF THOSE TWO PEOPLE WOULD YOU LIKE WITH YOU TODAY TO SWEETEN UP YOUR DAY AND REMIND YOU HOW SWEET LIFE AND YOU ARE?

WHAT QUALITIES DO THEY HAVE THAT YOU WOULD LIKE TO HAVE?
WHAT QUALITIES DO YOU HAVE THAT YOU ARE EITHER NOT SUFFICIENTLY AWARE OF OR ARE NOT PUTTING TO ENOUGH GOOD USE?
HOW CAN YOU PRACTISE AND LIVE THESE TODAY?

Sweetness

I want something sweet
No, not like food
Not like gifts.
I want something sweet

Something that smells like summer
Rests like lake water
Warms my skin like midday sun
Frees me like a swing

Something that sounds like whispers
Talks like peace
Comforts me like home
Cheers me like Maine

Something that loves like a puppy
Fights like a lion
Finds me in the dark
But puts me into hiding

I want something sweet
Maybe a tad bit complicated.
Maybe it'll be short-lived.
But it's happiness.
I want something sweet.

Maeve

Awareness

I have discovered
that a buttercup has five petals,
that several colours enliven a patch of moss
that grass comes in near - infinite variety and
that a swift flowing stream sings with an
astonishing range of voices

I came to know these things
when I slowed my walking pace
chose a narrow path with many turnings
and tuned all my senses to the world about me.

Cyril Lovett *Matters of the Heart*

The Sweetness of this World

WE CAN FEEL VERY PROUD OF OURSELVES AS HUMAN BEINGS. WHILE WE STARTED OUT IGNORANT ANIMALS, LIVING LIVES THAT WERE NASTY, BRUTISH AND SHORT, THANKS TO OUR BIG BRAINS, SCIENCE REPLACED SUPERSTITION AND TECHNOLOGY REPLACED RITUAL.

THE GODS ALWAYS PUNISHED HUBRIS.

We should remember that knowing is relationship and all relationships are live, on-going, infinite and mysterious experiences.

The more we know, the more we don't know.

We can handle our relationship with the universe in reverence and respect and doing this will give us better and more real knowledge.

See how much you can learn today from others and from your environment, no matter how certain you may feel about things.

LISTEN TO

LIFE IS A BITTERSWEET WALZE
BY
SEAN KEANE

SCAN WITH SMARTPHONE

The president of a large Banking corporation was in hospital gravely ill.

One of the Vice Presidents came to visit him and brought him a message.

"I bring you the good wishes of our Board of Directors, and the decision that you should be restored to health and live to be a hundred years.

That's an official resolution passed by a majority of 15 to 6 with 2 abstentions.

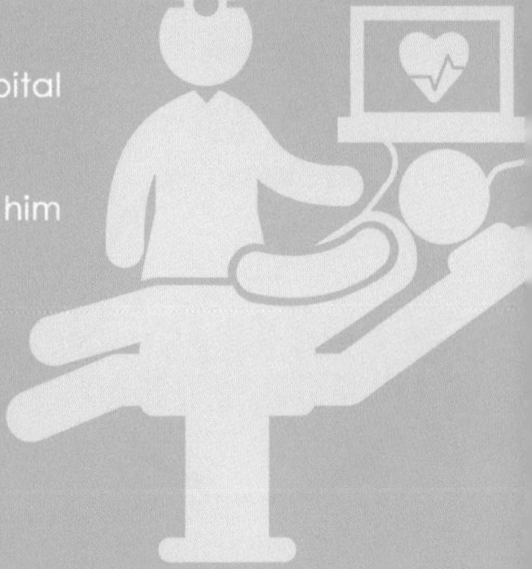

TODAY CAN YOU

TALK SWEETLY TO SOMEONE?
SMILE SWEETLY AT SOMEONE?
BE SWEET WITH SOMEONE?
LISTEN SWEETLY TO SOMEONE?
BE SWEETLY ON YOUR OWN?

SIMBA'S
TIP FOR TODAY

EAT WITH GUSTO
AND ENTHUSIASM.
STOP WHEN
YOU HAVE ENOUGH

YOUR BRAIN
TEASER FOR TODAY

Two men are talking.

One says to the other: "I have three sons whose ages I want you to ascertain from the following clues.

Stop me when you know their ages.

1. The sum of their ages is thirteen.
2. The product of their ages is the same as your age.
3. My oldest son weighs sixty-one pounds."

"Stop," says the second man. "I know their ages."

Do YOU?

When I am an old woman, I shall wear purple
with a red hat that doesn't go, and doesn't suit me.
And I shall spend my pension on brandy and summer gloves
and satin slippers, and say we've no money for butter.
I shall sit down on the pavement when I'm tired
and gobble up samples in shops and press alarm bells
and run my stick along the public railings
and make up for the sobriety of my youth.
I shall go out in my slippers in the rain
and pick the flowers in other people's gardens
and learn to spit.

You can wear terrible shirts and grow more fat
and eat three pounds of sausages at a go
or only bread and pickles for a week
and hoard pens and pencils and beer mats and things in boxes.
But now we must have clothes that keep us dry
and pay our rent and not swear in the street
and set a good example for the children.
We will have friends to dinner and read the papers.
But maybe I ought to practice a little now?
So people who know me are not too shocked and surprised
when suddenly I am old, and start to wear purple.

Jenny Joseph

THE HORRID VOICE OF SCIENCE

"THERE'S MACHINERY IN THE BUTTERFLY;
THERE'S A MAINSPRING TO THE BEE;
THERE'S HYDRAULICS TO A DAISY,
AND CONTRAPTIONS TO A TREE."

"IF WE COULD SEE THE BIRDIE
THAT MAKES THE CHIRPING SOUND
WITH X-RAY, SCIENTIFIC EYES,
WE COULD SEE THE WHEELS GO ROUND."

AND I HOPE ALL MEN
WHO THINK LIKE THIS
WILL SOON LIE UNDERGROUND.

YOUR
MANAGEMENT
MESSAGE
FOR
TODAY
IS

See your role as a KWA Manager – helping people to KNOW what is required, to WANT to do it and to be ABLE to do it – and as being about making everything better, every day.

This is perfectly in line with our vocation as human beings, with what makes us most human.

Once we do it, we will manage to be human.

LEADING BUSINESS ORGANISATIONS
WITH INTEGRITY AND EFFECTIVENESS

MANAGING
TO BE
HUMAN

BRIAN F. SMYTH

END OF DAY

HOPE YOU HAD A SWEET DAY.

WHO WAS SWEET TO YOU TODAY…EVEN IF THEY DIDN'T MEAN TO BE?

HOW WAS LIFE SWEET WITH YOU TODAY?

SWEET DREAMS!

DAY 17

The best way to treat obstacles is to use them as stepping-stones. Laugh at them, tread on them, and let them lead you to something better.

Enid Blyton

A RUSSIAN WORKERS DELEGATION WAS VISITING A FACTORY IN DETROIT. THE LEADER ASKED THE FOREMAN HOW MANY HOURS AN AMERICAN WORKER WORKED EACH WEEK.

"FORTY" SAID THE FOREMAN.

THE RUSSIAN SHOOK HIS HEAD. "IN MY COUNTRY,"
HE SAID, "THE AVERAGE WORKER WORKS SIXTY HOURS A WEEK."

"SIXTY HOURS?" EXCLAIMED THE FOREMAN.
"YOU'D NEVER GET THE MEN IN THIS FACTORY TO WORK THAT MUCH.
THEY'RE A BUNCH OF COMMIES."

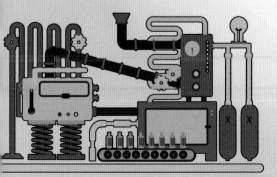

TODAY WILL BE A DAY WHERE YOU IDENTIFY AWKWARD THINGS, DIFFICULTIES, BLOCKS, THINGS THAT ARE NOT GOING AS WELL AS YOU WOULD WANT...YOU KNOW WHAT WE MEAN!

GOING FOR A WALK THERE CAN BE BRANCHES IN YOUR WAY, FENCES TO GET OVER, BROKEN PATHS, PEOPLE BLOCKING YOU, WEATHER ETC. ETC. LIFE CAN BE LIKE THAT TOO SOMETIMES.

TODAY MAY NOT BE ONE OF THOSE DAYS BUT YOU KNOW THEM AND SO TODAY YOU WILL THINK OF THESE AND ACTUALLY WELCOME THEM.

WHO KNOWS WHAT IS THE RIGHT PATH FOR YOU AND THAT BRANCH OR OBSTACLE MAY REDIRECT YOU OFF IN A DIFFERENT AND MAYBE BETTER WAY.

IN ANY CASE, YOU WILL LEARN TO SEE THESE THINGS IN A DIFFERENT LIGHT TODAY RATHER THAN SEEING THEM AS FRUSTRATIONS TO YOUR PLANS AND DESIGNS.

SO, SPOT ALL THE SET-BACKS, OBSTACLES AND ANNOYANCES TODAY AND SAY HELLO TO THEM WITH UNDERSTANDING AND A SMILE.

MUHAMMAD ALI SAID THAT OFTEN IT ISN'T THE MOUNTAINS AHEAD THAT WEAR YOU OUT, IT'S THE LITTLE PEBBLE IN YOUR SHOE SO WHETHER YOU ENCOUNTER MOUNTAINS OR PEBBLES TODAY, YOU HAVE SOME GREAT PEOPLE WHO WERE BORN ON THIS DAY TO HELP YOU ALONG.

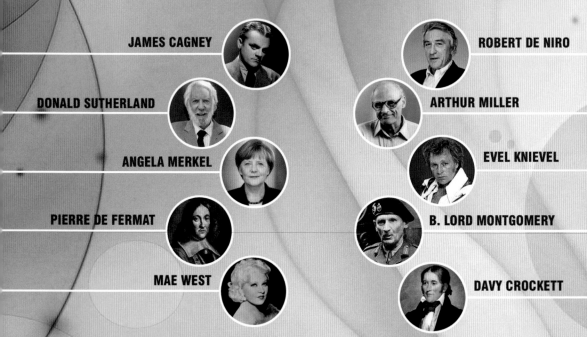

JAMES CAGNEY

ROBERT DE NIRO

DONALD SUTHERLAND

ARTHUR MILLER

ANGELA MERKEL

EVEL KNIEVEL

PIERRE DE FERMAT

B. LORD MONTGOMERY

MAE WEST

DAVY CROCKETT

HOW COULD YOU FAIL TO MAKE IT THROUGH THE DAY AND TO MAKE IT A GREAT DAY WITH SOME OF THESE COMPANIONS? SO WHO WILL YOU CHOOSE TO HAVE BESIDE YOU AND TO WHISPER IN YOUR EAR IF YOU COME ACROSS A DIFFICULTY OR SET-BACK?

WHAT QUALITIES DO THEY HAVE THAT YOU WOULD LIKE TO HAVE?
WHAT QUALITIES DO YOU HAVE THAT YOU ARE EITHER NOT SUFFICIENTLY AWARE OF OR ARE NOT PUTTING TO ENOUGH GOOD USE?
HOW CAN YOU PRACTISE AND LIVE THESE TODAY?

WHAT ARE TWO OR THREE THINGS HOLDING YOU BACK FROM ACHIEVING WHAT YOU REALLY WANT?

ARE ANY OF THESE OVER-COMEABLE?

If they are not,
then they are just reality!

Today identify one obstacle that is holding you
back and do something about it, or at least begin.
Find a gate somewhere today and:

- Open it
- Climb over it
- Leave it as it is.

CHOOSE ONE OR DO ALL THREE...
JUST FOR THE FUN OF IT.

There is a candle in your heart, ready to be kindled.
There is a void in your soul, ready to be filled.
You feel it, don't you?"

Rumi

WE CAN PURSUE SECURITY AT ALL COST AND SEEK OUT ANYTHING THAT FURTHERS OUR OWN INTEREST; FOR EXAMPLE, MONEY, STATUS, SECURITY, INFORMATION, AND POWER – ALL THOSE THINGS WE REGARD AS CRITICAL FOR OUR SECURITY AND INDEPENDENCE.

HOWEVER THIS CAN BE A VAIN PURSUIT.

The more we cooperate and inter-depend, the richer and more secure we are.

The more we are part of others and of everything, the less we need to compete, be better, superior, higher etc.

Have a look today at all the people on whom you depend and, rather than feeling bad about it, enjoy it and extend your dependence and interdependence.

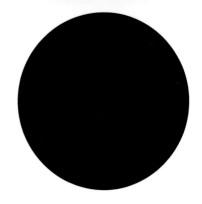

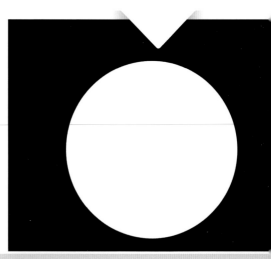

LISTEN TO

THE USES OF ADVERSITY
BY
DANIEL AMOS

SCAN WITH SMARTPHONE

Trees need not walk the earth
For beauty or for bread;
Beauty will come to them
Where they stand.
Here among the children of the sap
Is no pride of ancestry:
A birch may wear no less the morning
Than an oak.
Here are no heirlooms
Save those of loveliness,
In which each tree
Is kingly in its heritage of grace.
Here is but beauty's wisdom
In which all trees are wise.
Trees need not walk the earth
For beauty or for bread;
Beauty will come to them
In the rainbow—
The sunlight—
And the lilac-haunted rain;
And bread will come to them
As beauty came:
In the rainbow—
In the sunlight—
In the rain.

David Rosenthal

If you think you were beaten – you are!
If you think you dare not – you don't
If you'd like to win, but think you can't
It's almost a cinch you won't.
If you think you'll lose, you've lost,
For out in the world we find,
Success begins with the fellow's will,
It's all in the state of mind.
Life's battles don't always go
With the stronger or faster man,
But sooner or later the man who wins,
is the man who thinks he can.

Walter D Wintle

SIMBA'S
TIP FOR TODAY

WHEN SOMEONE IS HAVING A BAD DAY, BE SILENT, SIT CLOSE BY AND OFFER A GENTLE MUZZLE.

YOUR BRAIN TEASER FOR TODAY

More problems and obstacles!

The light has failed in your bedroom and you are going out to an important meeting where you will be on a podium talking. You have 10 grey socks and 20 blue socks in a drawer.

You are in the dark so, if you reach in to get a pair of socks, how many socks must you take out to be sure of having a pair of the same colour, that match?

YOUR
MANAGEMENT
MESSAGE
FOR
TODAY
IS

Giving people challenges is so easy to do. We are surrounded by challenges and problems and exciting opportunities.

People spend time away from work enjoying artificial challenges such as three mile races in athletics, climbing mountains, getting balls into holes in golf.

At work we have real challenges and some of us don't use them. Some managers can take all the burden on themselves, not just because they are so good and responsible, but because they enjoy the power, the sense of achievement, the ownership and responsibility, and the challenge. But, in the process, they reduce others to playing minor roles, making them feel bored and unimportant.

We can get people to want to work by running our companies in a truly creative and challenging way. We can invite all to help us to identify and take on the issues and problems that arise, and we can invite all to be alert and awake to all the options that surround us.

LEADING BUSINESS ORGANISATIONS
WITH INTEGRITY AND EFFECTIVENESS

MANAGING
TO BE
HUMAN

BRIAN F SMYTH

END OF DAY

HOPE YOU ARE NOT TOO BRUISED OR BATTERED FROM ALL THOSE OBSTACLES AND PROBLEMS.

HOPE TOO THAT YOU NOW SEE THESE SO CALLED OBSTACLES, NOT AS THINGS TO BE OVERCOME AS ONE WOULD AN ENEMY BUT PART OF A WORLD AND LIFE WITH WHICH YOU ARE IN DIALOGUE AND IN COLLABORATION.

REFLECT ON ANY OBSTACLE YOU DID NOT HANDLE SO WELL TODAY AND ONLY THINK OF HOW YOU FELT THEN. DO NOTHING ELSE.

DAY 18

Most people do not really want freedom, because freedom involves responsibility, and most people are frightened of responsibility.

Sigmund Freud

YOUR THEME FOR TODAY IS RESPONSIBILITY AND FREEDOM.

RESPONSIBILITY AND FREEDOM ARE ASSOCIATED AND IN FACT, GO HAND-IN-HAND.

THE MORE RESPONSIBILITY YOU TAKE FOR YOUR LIFE AND SITUATION, THE MORE REAL FREEDOM YOU WILL ENJOY. THE OPPOSITE IS, OF COURSE, TRUE TOO, AS WE KNOW FROM VICTIMS.

BE AWARE TODAY WHEN YOU ARE COMPLAINING OR 'GIVING OUT' ABOUT SOMETHING. YOU MAY BE DISEMPOWERING YOURSELF.... AND ANNOYING THOSE AROUND YOU.

TAKE AS MUCH RESPONSIBILITY AS POSSIBLE FOR EVERY SITUATION IN WHICH YOU FIND YOURSELF TODAY.

YOU WILL ENJOY TAKING RESPONSIBILITY TODAY AND FEELING THE POWER AND THE FREEDOM THAT THAT WILL GIVE YOU.

REAL FREEDOM

A former inmate of a Nazi concentration camp was visiting a friend who had shared the ordeal with him.

"Have you forgiven the Nazis?" He asked his friend.

"Yes."

"Well, I haven't. I'm still consumed with hatred for them."
"In that case," said his friend gently, "they still have you in prison."

The only kind of dignity which is genuine is that which is not diminished by the disrespect of others. You won't diminish the majesty of Niagara Falls by spitting in it.

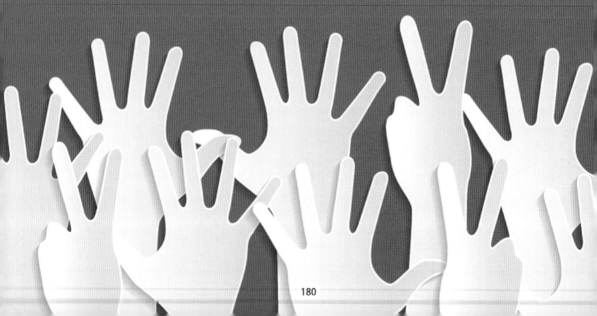

YOU HAVE SOME WONDERFULLY RESPONSIBLE PEOPLE ALONGSIDE YOU,
WHO WERE BORN ON THIS DATE, TO AID YOU IN BEING RESPONSIBLE...AND FREE.

HERBERT MARCUSE

ROBERT REDFORD

GRETA GARBO

JOHN TRAVOLTA

NELSON MANDELA

D.T.ZUZUKI

JOHN GLENN

MARTINA NAVRATILOVA

RICHARD BRANSON

PIERRE TRUDEAU

IMPRESSIVE LIST OF RESPONSIBLE AND FREE PEOPLE? WHICH TWO WOULD YOU LIKE
TO BE WITH YOU TODAY, REMINDING YOU IN EVERY SITUATION OF YOUR DAY, TO BE
RESPONSIBLE AND FREE?

WHAT QUALITIES DO THEY HAVE THAT YOU WOULD LIKE TO HAVE?
WHAT QUALITIES DO YOU HAVE THAT YOU ARE EITHER NOT SUFFICIENTLY AWARE OF OR ARE NOT
PUTTING TO ENOUGH GOOD USE?
HOW CAN YOU PRACTISE AND LIVE THESE TODAY?

Accountability

Folks ain't got no right to censuah othah folks about dey habits;
Him dat giv' de squir'ls de bushtails made de bobtails fu' de rabbits.
Him dat built de gread big mountains hollered out de little valleys,
Him dat made de streets an' driveways wasn't shamed to make de alleys.

We is all constructed diff'ent, d'ain't no two of us de same;
We cain't he'p ouah likes an' dislikes, ef we'se bad we ain't to blame.
Ef we 'se good, we need n't show off, case you bet it ain't ouah doin'
We gits into su'ttain channels dat we jes' cain't he'p pu'suin'.

But we all fits into places dat no othah ones could fill,
An' we does the things we has to, big er little, good er ill.
John cain't tek de place o' Henry, Su an' Sally ain't alike;
Bass ain't nuthin' like a suckah, chub ain't nuthin' like a pike.

When you come to think about it, how it 's all planned out it 's splendid.
Nuthin 's done er evah happens, 'dout hit 's somefin' dat 's intended;
Don't keer whut you does, you has to, an' hit sholy beats de dickens,--
Viney, go put on de kittle, I got one o' mastah's chickens.

Paul Laurence Dunbar

WE CAN SEE OURSELVES AS TOP OF THE HEAP AND NOT NEEDING THE HEAP ANY MORE, A SPECIAL KIND OF ANIMAL, THE APEX OF EVOLUTION, POSSESSING BRAINS THAT ALLOW THE CULTURAL AS WELL AS THE GENETIC TRANSFER OF INFORMATION.

YES WE ARE SPECIAL but intelligence is everywhere and in everything, communicating and working in and through everything.

We can give unique and wonderful expression to that endless process of communication by working in harmony with it rather than against it.

See how you continually depend on the intelligence of others and other things as well.

We can create the most wonderful gardens but it is the plants that provide the real creativity and the real wonder.

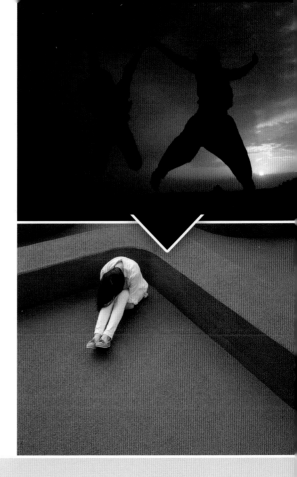

LISTEN TO

BLOWIN IN THE WIND
BY
BOB DYLAN

SCAN WITH SMARTPHONE

Look out for sharp or pointed things today and admire them and the power they have when you spot them.

Look at parents or mothers taking responsibility for their children's growth and welfare.

Find one truly responsible person in your life and identify with them and their qualities.

IS THERE SOMETHING THAT IS OF SOME IMPORTANCE TO YOU BUT THAT YOU HAVE BEEN LEAVING TO OTHERS?

IF SO, BEGIN TO TAKE RESPONSIBILITY FOR IT TODAY.

IS THERE SOME SITUATION WHERE YOU FEEL OR ARE ACTING A BIT LIKE A VICTIM?

IF SO PUT AN END TO IT, TAKE RESPONSIBILITY AND BECOME FREE.

BE REALLY ALERT TODAY IN EVERY MOMENT, IN EVERY SITUATION TODAY SO THAT YOU ARE RESPONDING REALLY WELL TO WHAT IS CALLED FOR.

SIMBA'S
TIP FOR TODAY

No matter how often you are scolded, don't buy into the guilt thing and pout – run right back and make friends.

YOUR BRAIN TEASER FOR TODAY

Frank, Greg, Harry, Iriving and Joseph are the competitors in a 100 metre race.

Frank beat Greg by as many places as Irving beat Joseph. Neither Harry nor Joseph was third or fifth.

IN WHAT ORDER DID THEY FINISH?

IN THE SUMMER OF 1946 THE RUMOUR OF A FAMINE SWEPT THROUGH A PROVINCE IN A SOUTH AMERICAN COUNTRY.

ACTUALLY THE CROPS WERE GROWING WELL, AND THE WEATHER WAS PERFECT FOR A BUMPER HARVEST.

BUT ON THE STRENGTH OF THAT RUMOUR, 20,000 SMALL FARMERS ABANDONED THEIR FARMS AND FLED TO THE CITIES. BECAUSE OF THEIR ACTION, THE CROPS FAILED, THOUSANDS STARVED AND THE RUMOUR ABOUT THE FAMINE PROVED TRUE.

"You were born with potential.
You were born with goodness and trust.
You were born with ideals and dreams.
You were born with greatness.
You were born with wings.
You are not meant for crawling, so don't.
You have wings.
Learn to use them and fly."
Rumi

YOUR MANAGEMENT MESSAGE FOR TODAY IS

The people that you influence are, in fact, your portals to the outside world. You touch, influence and impact the world through other people in your circle of influence.

Ultimately, how effective you are in the world will depend on the quality of the relationships you have with all these people. It is absolutely true that you are only as good as your relationships. It is an enormous responsibility and privilege to be in such a position and one we should not take lightly.

However, it is one we should welcome and feel immensely grateful for.

DING BUSINESS ORGANISATIONS
H INTEGRITY AND EFFECTIVENESS

MANAGING
TO BE
HUMAN

BRIAN F. SMYTH

END OF DAY

WHAT DO YOU FEEL GOOD ABOUT TODAY THAT YOU TOOK RESPONSIBILITY FOR?

THINK OF SOME MOMENTS WHEN YOU FELT REALLY FREE TODAY.

WHATEVER HAPPENED OR DIDN'T HAPPEN TODAY, REMEMBER THAT TOMORROW
YOU HAVE A WHOLE NEW DAY TO CONTINUE AND TO DO EVEN BETTER THAN
TODAY....IN THIS AND IN EVERYTHING.

DAY 19

Nothing in the world can take the place of persistence.
Talent will not: nothing is more common than unsuccessful people with talent.
Genius will not: unrewarded genius is almost a proverb.
Education will not: the world is full of educated derelicts.

Chay Blyth

HOW IS YOUR MOOD TODAY?
(CHOOSE COLOUR, ANIMAL, OBJECT, PERSON)

WHAT DOES THIS MOOD MEAN FOR HOW YOU LIVE TODAY?

WHAT MIGHT YOU NEED TO WATCH FOR?

WHEN HAVE YOU GIVEN UP IN THE PAST BEFORE YOU OUGHT TO HAVE?

THINK OF ONE AREA IN YOUR LIFE WHERE YOU REALLY NEED TO PERSIST AND NOT GIVE UP FOR GOOD REASONS.

WHAT ARE SOME THINGS THAT ARE WITHIN YOUR REACH AND YOU ONLY HAVE TO MAKE ONE MORE EFFORT TO GET THERE?

SOME REALLY GREAT AND PERSISTENT PEOPLE WERE BORN ON THIS VERY DATE.
THEY WILL BE WITH YOU TO URGE YOU ON AND TO KEEP GOING.

DOLLY PARTON

MAMA CASS

EDGAR ALLEN POE

NICOLAS COPERNICUS

WILLIAM GOLDING

JOHN LE CARRÉ

PAULO FREIRE

EVANDER HOLLYFIELD

BRIAN EPSTEIN

PETER DRUCKER

WHICH TWO OR THREE OF THESE WOULD YOU MOST LIKE TO BE OR FOLLOW TODAY?

WHAT QUALITIES DO THEY HAVE THAT YOU WOULD LIKE TO HAVE?
WHAT QUALITIES DO YOU HAVE THAT YOU ARE EITHER NOT SUFFICIENTLY AWARE OF OR ARE NOT
PUTTING TO ENOUGH GOOD USE?
HOW CAN YOU PRACTISE AND LIVE THESE TODAY?

Patience, Persistence .... and ... Silence

A traveller lost in the desert despaired of ever finding water. He struggled up one hilltop, then another and another in the hope of sighting a stream somewhere. He kept looking in every direction with no success.

As he staggered onwards his foot caught on a dry bush and he stumbled to the ground. That's where he lay, with no energy even to rise, no desire to struggle any more, no hope of surviving this ordeal.

As he lay there, helpless and dejected, he suddenly became aware of the silence of the desert. On all sides a majestic stillness reigned, undisturbed by the slightest sound. Suddenly he raised his head. He had heard something. Something so faint that only the sharpest ear and the deepest silence would lead to its detection: the sound of running water.

Heartened by the hope that the sound aroused in him, he rose and kept moving until he arrived at a stream of fresh, cool water.

When you have gone so far that you can't manage one more step, then you've gone just half the distance that you are capable of.

Greenland proverb

'YES WE CAN'. WE CAN BELIEVE THAT THE ONLY LIMIT TO OUR ABILITY TO DO SO IS THAT AMOUNT OF FORCE WE CAN HARNESS AND THE PRECISION WITH WHICH WE CAN APPLY IT.

YES, WE DO HAVE A LOT OF POWER but the force we bring to bear can be counterproductive and weaken us and our efforts.

All we do is only truly effective when done in a healthy and harmonious relationship with others, our environment and our universe.

If you believe this you will become ever so much more powerful as you unite your power with that of others.

Why not find opportunities to do that today. There will be lots of them.

LISTEN TO
DAYDREAMER
BY
ADELE

SCAN WITH SMARTPHONE

SIMBA'S
TIP FOR TODAY

Whatever you do, **BE LOYAL!**

YOUR BRAIN
TEASER FOR TODAY

During the Middle Ages, a Nordic King had a problem. His sons were good friends, and the king wanted to make sure that they would have no cause for jealousy after his death over the division of his property.

He didn't want to provide in his will merely that the possessions were to be divided equally, lest his sons start quarrelling over what each was to get.

Finally the King thought of a foolproof yet simple way of providing for absolutely equal distribution of his possessions.

What did he write in his will?

We live in deeds, not years; in thoughts, not breaths

We live in deeds, not years; in thoughts, not breaths;
In feelings, not in figures on a dial.

We should count time by heart-throbs. He most lives
Who thinks most, feels the noblest, acts the best.
And he whose heart beats quickest lives the longest:
Lives in one hour more than in years do some
Whose fat blood sleeps as it slips along their veins.

Life's but a means unto an end; that end,
Beginning, mean, and end to all things-God.

The dead have all the glory of the world.

Philip James Bailey

YOUR
MANAGEMENT
MESSAGE
FOR
TODAY
IS

Being true to our humanity is critical for our happiness and well-being, and our difficulty in achieving this affects every part of our lives and every part of our world.

Our frequent failure to behave, lead and manage in a truly human way is of increasing concern to more and more people.

LEADING BUSINESS ORGANISATIONS
WITH INTEGRITY AND EFFECTIVENESS

MANAGING
TO BE
HUMAN

BRIAN F. SMYTH

END OF DAY

ONE THING YOU LEARNED ABOUT YOURSELF TODAY.

ONE THING YOU WILL HANDLE BETTER TOMORROW OR IN FUTURE.

ONE THING YOU ARE GRATEFUL FOR FROM TODAY.

ONE ACTION YOU TOOK TODAY WHEN YOU DIDN'T FEEL LIKE DOING IT…AT ALL.

DAY 20

I don't believe an accident of birth makes people sisters or brothers. It makes them siblings, gives them mutuality of parentage. Sisterhood and brotherhood is a condition people have to work at.

Maya Angelou

COUNTING YOUR LOSSES –
LOSING 'DEAR' ONES

At the funeral of a very wealthy man,
a stranger was seen mourning and
weeping as loudly as the others.

The officiating priest walked up to him
and asked,

"My sympathies.
You must be a close relative
of the deceased."

"No, I am not."

"Then why are you crying?"

"That's why."

TODAY IS ABOUT THOSE PEOPLE WHO ARE CLOSEST
TO YOU – YOUR BROTHER OR SISTER OR PARTNER
OR FRIEND OR COLLEAGUE.

MAYBE THEY ARE NOT AWARE OF HOW IMPORTANT
THEY ARE TO YOU.

MAYBE YOU ARE NOT AWARE OF HOW IMPORTANT
THEY ARE TO YOU!

MAYBE YOU ARE NOT AWARE OF HOW IMPORTANT
YOU ARE TO THEM!'

BE GRATEFUL…WHETHER YOU EXPRESS IT OR NOT.

DO YOU EVER THINK OF HOW MANY PEOPLE THINK
OF YOU EVERY DAY WITHOUT YOU KNOWING IT.

THINK OF ONE BIG ACHIEVEMENT
IN YOUR LIFE SO
FAR ABOUT WHICH YOU FEEL
GOOD.

YOU ARE SHARING TODAY WITH SOME LOVELY FRIENDS WHO WERE BORN ON THIS DATE

SOPHIA LOREN

BO DEREK

JUAN MONTOYA

ROBERT KENNEDY

SIDNEY POITIER

SERGEI RACHMANINOV.

JOAN MIRO

DAVID BOHM

BENOIT MANDELBROT

URI GELLER

WHO WOULD YOU LIKE AS YOUR FRIEND TO ACCOMPANY YOU TODAY?

WHAT QUALITIES DO THEY HAVE THAT YOU WOULD LIKE TO HAVE?
WHAT QUALITIES DO YOU HAVE THAT YOU ARE EITHER NOT SUFFICIENTLY AWARE OF OR ARE NOT PUTTING TO ENOUGH GOOD USE?
HOW CAN YOU PRACTISE AND LIVE THESE TODAY?

IT IS SO EASY TO BELIEVE THAT BECAUSE WE ARE FUNDAMENTALLY SEPARATE FROM EACH OTHER, MY SELF INTEREST IS VERY LIKELY AT THE EXPENSE OF YOUR SELF-INTEREST.

NO! This is probably one of the biggest mistakes or lies there is.

As we are all part of the one and of each other, what is less for one is less for the other and for all.

The better the whole, the better the other and the better you are.

See if you can find examples, lots of them, today where this is true. They are all around you.

LISTEN TO

HE AIN'T HEAVY, HE'S MY BROTHER
BY
THE HOLLIES

SCAN WITH SMARTPHONE

Contact someone today that you haven't
been in touch with for a while.

What do you see in the sky today?
Stay in touch with the sky today whatever is happening or you see.

SMELL SOMETHING NICE TODAY – PERFUME, FOOD, FLOWER.

FEEL WARMTH TODAY...FROM THE SUN, FROM A FIRE, FROM A FRIEND, FROM THE UNIVERSE.

"DO YOU KNOW WHAT YOU ARE?
YOU ARE A MANUSCRIPT OF A DIVINE LETTER.
YOU ARE A MIRROR REFLECTING A NOBLE FACE.
THIS UNIVERSE IS NOT OUTSIDE OF YOU.
LOOK INSIDE YOURSELF;
EVERYTHING THAT YOU WANT,
YOU ARE ALREADY THAT."

RUMI

SIMBA'S
TIP FOR TODAY

... from his book: *A Dog's Life or God's Life?*

No matter
what happens
always be true to
who you really are.

**YOUR BRAIN
TEASER FOR TODAY**

$$\begin{array}{r} SEND \\ + MORE \\ \hline MONEY \end{array}$$

203

UPHILL

Does the road wind up-hill all the way?
Yes, to the very end.
Will the day's journey take the whole long day?
From morn to night, my friend.

But is there for the night a resting-place?
A roof for when the slow dark hours begin.
May not the darkness hide it from my face?
You cannot miss that inn.

Shall I meet other wayfarers at night?
Those who have gone before.
Then must I knock, or call when just in sight?
They will not keep you standing at that door.

Shall I find comfort, travel-sore and weak?
Of labour you shall find the sum.
Will there be beds for me and all who seek?
Yea, beds for all who come.

Christina Rosetti

I will not die an unlived life
I will not live in fear
of falling or catching fire.
I choose to inhabit my days,
to allow my living to open me,
to make me less afraid,
more accessible,
to loosen my heart
until it becomes a wing,
a torch, a promise.
I choose to risk my significance;
to live so that which came to me as seed
goes to the next as blossom
and that which came to me as blossom,
goes on as fruit.

— Dawna Markova

YOUR MANAGEMENT MESSAGE FOR TODAY IS

It is possible to act in a human way all the time (in work situations) and doing so is helpful for everyone involved, and leads to better and more successful organizations and businesses. The roots of our humanity and goodness go very deep.

We cannot turn a blind eye to them. Unfortunately, other so-called 'goods', such as a narrow version of what success means for the organization or for ourselves, can override our deepest human instincts.

These can be regarded as not relevant for the Business, or, while important, have to be sacrificed for the so-called good of the Business. Mantras like: 'Business is Business' can supersede our values and what is right. The fact is, there is no need to take such a stance and no real benefit for the organization or for ourselves from doing so.

ADING BUSINESS ORGANISATIONS
ITH INTEGRITY AND EFFECTIVENESS

MANAGING TO BE HUMAN

BRIAN F. SMYTH

Happy the man, and happy he alone,
He who can call today his own:
He who, secure within, can say,
Tomorrow do thy worst, for I have lived today.

Be fair or foul or rain or shine
The joys I have possessed, in spite of fate, are mine.
Not heaven itself upon the past has power,
But what has been, has been, and I have had my hour

John Dryden

END OF DAY

THINK OF ONE BRAVE OR COURAGEOUS THING YOU DID TODAY.

WHERE MIGHT YOU HAVE BEEN MORE COURAGEOUS?

DAY 21

Once the realization is accepted that even between the closest human beings infinite distances continue to exist, a wonderful living side by side can grow up, if they succeed in loving the distance between them which makes it possible for each to see the other against the sky.

Rainer Maria Rilke

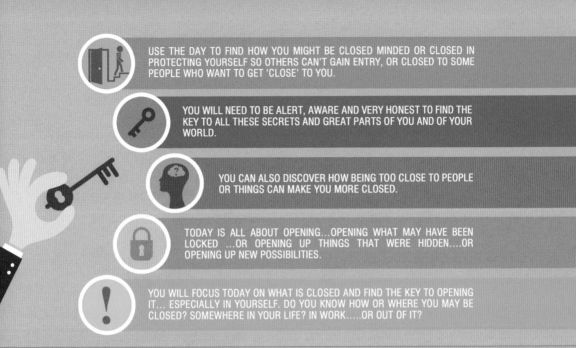

USE THE DAY TO FIND HOW YOU MIGHT BE CLOSED MINDED OR CLOSED IN PROTECTING YOURSELF SO OTHERS CAN'T GAIN ENTRY, OR CLOSED TO SOME PEOPLE WHO WANT TO GET 'CLOSE' TO YOU.

YOU WILL NEED TO BE ALERT, AWARE AND VERY HONEST TO FIND THE KEY TO ALL THESE SECRETS AND GREAT PARTS OF YOU AND OF YOUR WORLD.

YOU CAN ALSO DISCOVER HOW BEING TOO CLOSE TO PEOPLE OR THINGS CAN MAKE YOU MORE CLOSED.

TODAY IS ALL ABOUT OPENING...OPENING WHAT MAY HAVE BEEN LOCKED ...OR OPENING UP THINGS THAT WERE HIDDEN....OR OPENING UP NEW POSSIBILITIES.

YOU WILL FOCUS TODAY ON WHAT IS CLOSED AND FIND THE KEY TO OPENING IT... ESPECIALLY IN YOURSELF. DO YOU KNOW HOW OR WHERE YOU MAY BE CLOSED? SOMEWHERE IN YOUR LIFE? IN WORK.....OR OUT OF IT?

LEARNING FROM LIFE

A couple of hunters chartered a plane to fly them into forest territory. Two weeks later the pilot came to take them back. He took a look at the animals they had shot and said, "This plane won't take more than one wild buffalo. You have to leave the other behind."

"But last year the pilot let us take two in a plane this size," the hunters protested.
The pilot was doubtful, but finally he said, "Well, if you did it last year I guess we can do it again."

So the the plane took off with the three men and two buffaloes.
But it couldn't gain height and crashed into a neighbouring hill.

The men climbed out and looked around. One hunter said to the other,
"Where do you think we are?" The other inspected the surroundings and said,
"I think we're about two miles to the left of where we crashed last year."

YES, THERE IS A LOT HERE AND NOT ALL EASY STUFF. HOWEVER, YOU ARE NOT ALONE. YOU WILL HAVE SOME WONDERFUL PEOPLE WITH YOU TODAY TO HELP YOU OPEN UP TO WONDERFUL THINGS IN YOU AND IN YOUR WORLD.

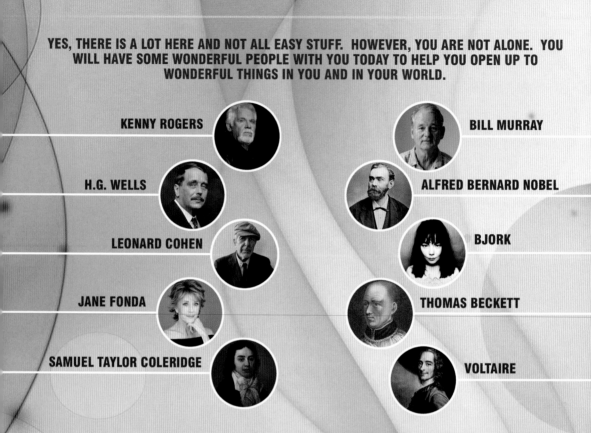

KENNY ROGERS

BILL MURRAY

H.G. WELLS

ALFRED BERNARD NOBEL

LEONARD COHEN

BJORK

JANE FONDA

THOMAS BECKETT

SAMUEL TAYLOR COLERIDGE

VOLTAIRE

SOME VERY OPEN AND COURAGEOUS AND FUN PEOPLE IN THERE TO HELP YOU OPEN. BUT, JUST CHOOSE NO MORE THAN TWO. YOU WILL NEED MORE OF THESE NEXT MONTH.

WHAT QUALITIES DO THEY HAVE THAT YOU WOULD LIKE TO HAVE?
WHAT QUALITIES DO YOU HAVE THAT YOU ARE EITHER NOT SUFFICIENTLY AWARE OF OR ARE NOT PUTTING TO ENOUGH GOOD USE?
HOW CAN YOU PRACTISE AND LIVE THESE TODAY?

BE ALERT FOR SOMETHING NEW
AND GREAT TODAY EACH TIME

You open a door

You open your computer

You open a letter

You open your eyes

You open your mind

Find one such key for some part of your life…find it…it is there and it will unlock wonderful things.

You open your heart to someone.

Look at some keys you have and all the magic they can unlock.

This being human is a guest-house.
Every morning a new arrival.
A joy, a depression, a meanness,
some momentary awareness comes
as an unexpected visitor.
Welcome and entertain them all!
Even if they're a crowd of sorrows,
Who violently sweep your house
empty of its furniture.

Still, treat each guest honorably.
He may be clearing you out
for some new delight.
The dark thought, the shame, the malice,
meet them at the door laughing,
and invite them in.
Be grateful for whoever comes,
because each has been sent
as a guide from beyond.

Jalrudin Rumi

WE ARE UNIQUE – WE ARE OFTEN TOLD - IN HAVING A SOUL (IN THE RELIGIOUS VIEW) OR A RATIONAL MIND (IN THE SCIENTIFIC VIEW).

YES, WE ARE UNIQUE and can share in and express the meaning and soul at work in everything in very special ways.

Everything rejoices in our ability to express, admire and celebrate the wonder at work in everything.

Yes we are unique but not alone.

Find just one example of YOUR uniqueness today, of one thing, one contribution that only YOU can make.

Then make it today and everyday.

LISTEN TO

ONE STEP CLOSER
BY
U2

SIMBA'S TIP FOR TODAY

... from his book: *Getting Access to a Dog's Life*

Don't worry when they close the door on you.

It gets you exploring other interesting places.

YOUR BRAIN TEASER FOR TODAY

WHAT DO THE FOLLOWING WORDS HAVE IN COMMON

- DEFT
- FIRST
- CALMNESS
- CANOPY
- LAUGHING
- STUPID
- CRABCAKE
- HIJACK

213

YOUR MANAGEMENT MESSAGE FOR TODAY IS

We need to establish systems, forums and meetings by which to pursue and get feedback and seek these out.

Such openness to feedback will not happen by default. We have to set up the mechanisms that will seek it out and protect them against assault from all sides. The great opponent of feedback is pride and the ego.

We don't like to be wrong and we forget that we are always wrong. Feedback will allow us to get closer to being right more often.

LEADING BUSINESS ORGANISATIONS
WITH INTEGRITY AND EFFECTIVENESS

MANAGING
TO BE
HUMAN

BRIAN F. SMYTH

Look for keys,
locked things,
passwords today
and feel the magic
they hide and protect.

When one door of opportunity
closes, another opens, but often
we look so long at the closed
door that we do not see the one
which has been opened for us.

END OF DAY

WHAT IS ONE OPENING FROM TODAY THAT YOU WELCOMED AND ENJOYED?

WHAT ARE SOME THINGS OR AREAS THAT REMAIN LOCKED BUT FOR WHICH YOU WILL FIND AND USE THE KEY...VERY SOON.

IS THERE ONE PERSON TO WHOM YOU GOT A LITTLE CLOSER TODAY?

SAY THANKS FOR CLOSE FRIENDS AND FORGIVE YOURSELF WHERE YOU FAILED TO OPEN SUFFICIENTLY TO THEM.

WAS THERE ANY SITUATION TODAY WHEN YOU WERE CLOSED OR CLOSED MINDED? IF SO, REPLAY IT IN YOUR HEAD AS YOU WOULD HAVE LIKED AND WOULD LIKE TO HANDLE IT – IN LINE WITH THE KIND OF PERSON YOU REALLY ARE AND WANT TO BE.

DAY 22

Whoever creates trust and higher purpose amongst their people gets unparalleled levels of support for common goals.

Anon

Today is all about trust…trust in others, trust in the whole world and trust in yourself.

Of course, there is no guarantee that trusting will pay off; like all of life it is a gamble but one that creates a good response.

The more you trust, the more you will trust….because you will see the results from it.

Already you are trusting so many things every day: trusting the sun will 'rise', trusting the brakes on your car will work, trusting the environment will provide enough oxygen for you to breathe and live, trusting a person in another car will stop at a red light and trusting so many people around you to do what they believe is right and good and will not let you down.

We will want you to take some risks in trusting as well. No risk, no reward, but you won't lose out. Ready for all that? Ready for a day of trusting the world and others?

GETTING OUT OF THE WAY

Said a world-famous violinist about his success in playing Beethoven's violin Concerto:

"I have splendid music, a splendid violin and a splendid bow. All I need to do is bring them together, trust and get out of the way."

AND, YOU WILL NOT BE ALONE IN THIS.
SOME WONDERFUL AND TRUSTING PEOPLE CAME INTO THE WORLD ON THIS DAY.

ALFRED TENNYSON

ANDREA BOCELLI

LUCILLE BALL

FRANZ LISZT

ROBERT MITCHUM

BERT TRAUTMANN

FREDDIE LAKER

DORY PREVIN

NICK CAVE

ANDY WARHOL

EASY TO TRUST IN THE COMPANY OF SOME OF THESE! WHO WILL YOU CHOOSE TO BE WITH YOU TODAY TO HELP YOU TRUST MORE?
JUST ONE OR TWO OF THEM FOR THIS MONTH.

WHAT QUALITIES DO THEY HAVE THAT YOU WOULD LIKE TO HAVE?
WHAT QUALITIES DO YOU HAVE THAT YOU ARE EITHER NOT SUFFICIENTLY AWARE OF OR ARE NOT PUTTING TO ENOUGH GOOD USE?
▶ ▶ ▶ ▶ ▶ ▶ HOW CAN YOU PRACTISE AND LIVE THESE TODAY? ▶ ▶ ▶

TRUST

It's like so many other things in life
to which you must say no or yes.
So you take your car to the new mechanic.
Sometimes the best thing to do is trust.
The package left with the disreputable-looking
clerk, the check gulped by the night deposit,
the envelope passed by dozens of strangers—
all show up at their intended destinations.
The theft that could have happened doesn't.
Wind finally gets where it was going
through the snowy trees, and the river, even
when frozen, arrives at the right place.
And sometimes you sense how faithfully your life
is delivered, even though you can't read the address.

THOMAS R. SMITH

YOUR ACTIVITIES FOR TODAY

TAKE TWO RISKS TODAY TRUSTING SOMEONE.

FIND SOME SITUATIONS IN YOUR LIFE WHERE YOU ARE NOT TRUSTING ENOUGH.

FIND EXAMPLES FROM NATURE OR WHEREVER, WHERE TRUST IS STRONGLY IN EVIDENCE.

CLOSE YOUR EYES AND WALK AROUND A ROOM TRUSTING YOURSELF.

THINK OF SOMEONE IN YOUR LIFE WHO NEEDS YOUR TRUST.

SEE HOW LONG YOU CAN STAND ON ONE
FOOT AND TRUST YOUR SENSE OF BALANCE.

"Oh soul,
you worry too much.
You have seen your own strength.
You have seen your own beauty.
You have seen your golden wings.
Of anything less,
why do you worry?
You are in truth
the soul, of the soul, of the soul."

Rumi

THERE ARE DAYS WHEN IT IS EASY TO BELIEVE THAT THERE IS NO PURPOSE TO LIFE, ONLY CAUSE. THAT THE UNIVERSE IS AT BOTTOM BLIND AND DEAD.

BUT you can get beyond this and stick to the truth that meaning lies at the heart of everything and is what moves everything from within.

We – you – are creatures, lovers of meaning.

Find the meaning behind all you do today. It is your connection to the overall and fundamental meaning.

LISTEN TO

TRUST
BY
KRISTENE MUELLER

SCAN WITH SMARTPHONE

YOUR COLOR FOR TODAY IS ORANGE

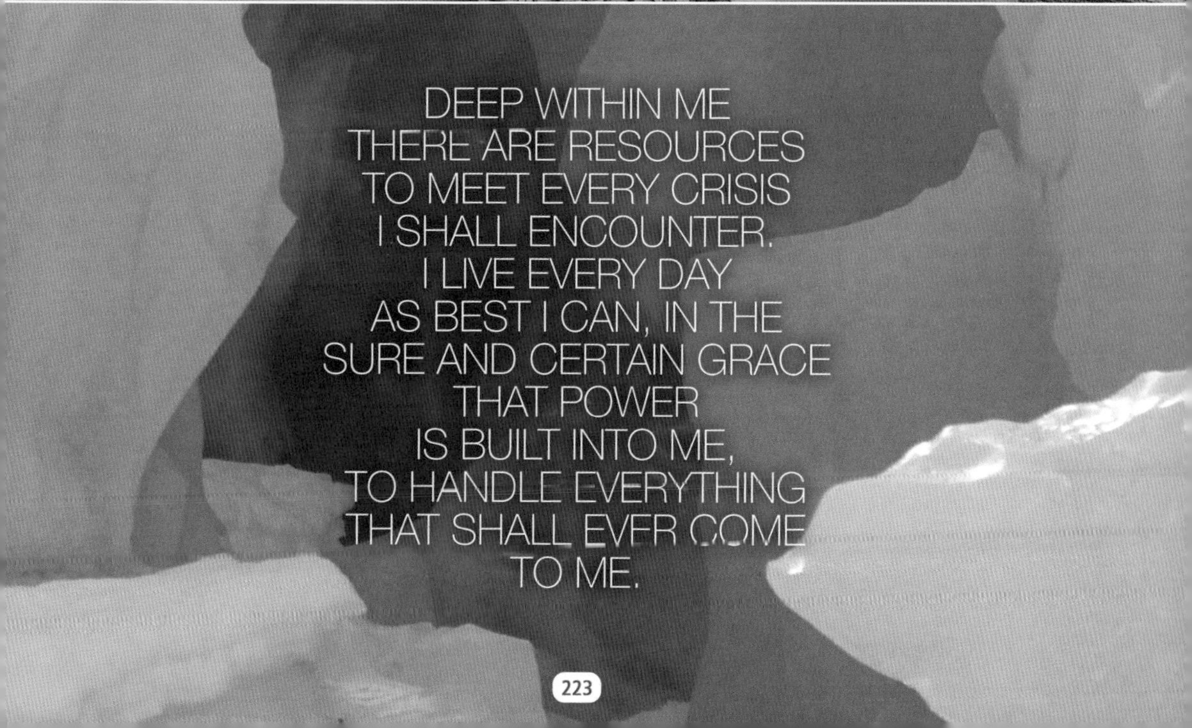

DEEP WITHIN ME
THERE ARE RESOURCES
TO MEET EVERY CRISIS
I SHALL ENCOUNTER.
I LIVE EVERY DAY
AS BEST I CAN, IN THE
SURE AND CERTAIN GRACE
THAT POWER
IS BUILT INTO ME,
TO HANDLE EVERYTHING
THAT SHALL EVER COME
TO ME.

SIMBA'S
TIP FOR TODAY

Never worry if people leave you behind; they always come back

YOUR BRAIN TEASER FOR TODAY

You are taking a part time job in a Company for which you will receive €10,000 a year.

On the first day, the manager in the Company calls you in and asks you whether you would like a raise of €1,000 every year, or €250 every six months.

WHICH WILL YOU DECIDE TO ACCEPT?

YOUR
MANAGEMENT
MESSAGE
FOR
TODAY
IS

This can sound contradictory, as management is often seen to be all about control. While this is true to an extent, we do have to learn to control the right things.

We can never really be in control of everything and our best way of dealing with the uncontrollable is to trust people to each look after their particular piece of the wider picture. In that way we have a network of management which has a far greater capacity to control and we have to trust them and to let go.

It is a vicious circle in the sense that the less we trust people, the less trustworthy people will be and the more we will be confirmed in our stance not to trust. We all know that risk and reward ride side by side. And if you avoid one the other will also pass you by. How easy is it for you to trust people?

DING BUSINESS ORGANISATIONS
TH INTEGRITY AND EFFECTIVENESS

MANAGING
TO BE
HUMAN

BRIAN F. SMYTH

HAVE PEOPLE DISAPPOINTED YOU OR LET YOU DOWN IN THE PAST?

DO YOU BELIEVE IN TAKING RISKS WITH PEOPLE?

HOW TRUSTED DO YOUR PEOPLE FEEL?

ARE THEY TRUSTWORTHY?

HOW AND IN WHAT AREAS COULD YOU TAKE MORE RISKS WITH PEOPLE AND CONTROL LESS?

DO YOU REALLY BELIEVE THAT THE GREATEST GIFT YOU CAN GIVE YOUR PEOPLE IS TO TRUST THEM?

END OF DAY

HOPE YOU HAD SOME GREAT EXPERIENCES FROM FEELING THE POWER OF TRUST TODAY.

APPARENTLY, THE WORDS 'DON'T FEAR' APPEAR OVER 150 TIMES IN THE NEW TESTAMENT IN THE BIBLE. FOR SOME REASON!

SOON YOU WILL CLOSE YOUR EYES AND ENTRUST YOURSELF TO SLEEP AND BE WELL LOOKED AFTER, AS YOU ALWAYS ARE.

DAY 23

Whatever you can do or dream you can, begin it. Boldness has genius, power and magic in it. Begin it now.

Goethe

THE DANGER OF LOOKING
FOR SECURITY AND PLAYING IT SAFE

ONE OF THE MEN WHO ACCOMPANIED
CHRISTOPHER COLUMBUS ON HIS EXPEDITION
TO THE NEW WORLD SPENT ALL THE TIME
WORRYING THAT HE MIGHT NOT GET BACK IN
TIME TO SUCCEED THE OLD VILLAGE TAILOR
AND SOMEONE ELSE MIGHT SNATCH THE JOB.

*"To succeed in an adventure and in the
adventure of life, one must have one's mind set
on getting the most out of life. Settling for trifles
like wealth, fame, comfort, success and
popularity just won't work."*

ANTHONY DE MELLO

Today is about adventure and
being venturous.
You may not feel a bit like that today but
maybe that is the best time to look at what
this would mean for you and why
it is valuable and important.

How has your life been
an adventure to date?
What are some of the main
chapters in that adventure story?

What will the next chapter be?

Will you wait for it to come
along or go looking for it?

Keep this to the forefront of
your mind during the day and do
at least one thing about awakening
the adventure in your life.

Allegedly, in some Tsunami, a man refused to abandon his house when floods were rising and let his family escape. "I put my faith in God," he said. "He will look after me."

People in a small boat passing by shouted to him to get in the boat but he refused and shouted to them that he had put his faith in God and God would look after him.

Later a ferry passed by and told him to quickly get on board but they got the same response.

Finally, the water had risen so high that he was on the roof. A helicopter came along and dropped a rope ladder to him to climb up but he waved it and them away telling them again that he had put his faith in God and that God would look after him.

He drowned and went to heaven and, when he met God he said to him: "You're some friend. I put all my faith in you and you did nothing."

"What do you mean, I did nothing," God replied. I sent you a boat, a ferry and a helicopter, and you took none of them."

WATCH FOR YOUR BOATS ETC.
TODAY AND EVERY DAY.
THEY WILL ALWAYS BE AROUND.

TODAY MAY BE EXCITING AND YOU MAY FEEL A BIT NERVOUS, BUT YOU HAVE VERY ADVENTUROUS AND BRAVE PEOPLE WHO WERE BORN ON THIS DAY TO ENCOURAGE YOU TO BE ADVENTUROUS.

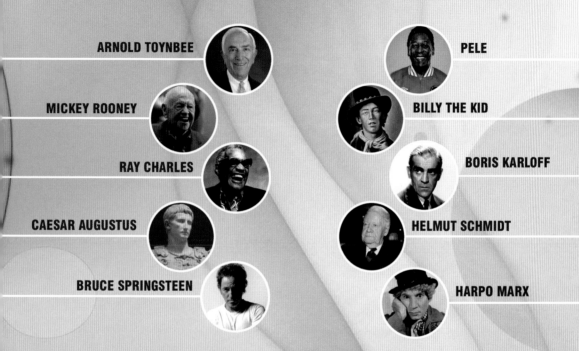

ARNOLD TOYNBEE

PELE

MICKEY ROONEY

BILLY THE KID

RAY CHARLES

BORIS KARLOFF

CAESAR AUGUSTUS

HELMUT SCHMIDT

BRUCE SPRINGSTEEN

HARPO MARX

SOME BRAVE AND ADVENTUROUS PEOPLE TO KEEP YOU COMPANY ON THIS YOUR ADVENTUROUS 23. CHOOSE ONE OR TWO WHO WILL BELIEVE IN YOU AND URGE YOU TO GO AFTER YOUR REAL ADVENTURE.

WHAT QUALITIES DO THEY HAVE THAT YOU WOULD LIKE TO HAVE?
WHAT QUALITIES DO YOU HAVE THAT YOU ARE EITHER NOT SUFFICIENTLY AWARE OF OR ARE NOT PUTTING TO ENOUGH GOOD USE?
HOW CAN YOU PRACTISE AND LIVE THESE TODAY?

For ages you have come and gone courting this delusion.
For ages you have run from the pain
and forfeited the ecstasy.
So come, return to the root of the root of your own soul.

Although you appear in earthly form
Your essence is pure Consciousness.
You are the fearless guardian of Divine Light.
So come, return to the root of the root of your own soul.

When you lose all sense of self
the bonds of a thousand chains will vanish.
Lose yourself completely,
Return to the root of the root of your own soul.

You descended from Adam, by the pure Word of God,
but you turned your sight to the empty show of this world.
Alas, how can you be satisfied with so little?
So come, return to the root of the root of your own soul.

Why are you so enchanted by this world
when a mine of gold lies within you?
Open your eyes and come ---
Return to the root of the root of your own soul.

Rumi

HOPE YOU CAN RETURN TO THE ROOT
OF YOUR OWN SOUL TODAY
AND FREE YOURSELF FROM TIES
THAT ARE HOLDING YOU BACK...
ONLY THOSE ONES.

BE THEY 'REAL' OR REAL IN YOUR HEAD

To laugh is to risk appearing the fool.
To weep is to risk appearing sentimental.
To reach out for another is to risk involvement.
To expose your feelings is to risk exposing your true self.
To place your ideas and your dreams before a crowd is to risk their loss.
To love is to risk not being loved in return.
To live is to risk dying.
To hope is to risk despair.
To try is to risk failure.

But risks must be taken, for the greater hazard is to risk nothing.
The person who risks nothing, does nothing, has nothing and is nothing.
He may avoid suffering and sorrow but he cannot learn,
change, grow, love, live.

Chained by his attitude, he is a slave, he has forfeited freedom.
Only a person who risks is free.

Now and Then

Did we but know what lurks beyond the NOW;
Could we but see what the dim future hides;
Had we some power occult that would us show
The joy and sorrow which in THEN abides;
Would life be happier, - or less fraught with woe,
Did we but know?

I long, yet fear to pierce those clouds ahead; -
To solve life's secrets, - learn what means this death.
Are fresh joys waiting for the silent dead?
Or do we perish with a fleeting breath?
If not; then whither will the spirit go?
Did we but know.

'Tis all a mist. Reason can naught explain,
We dream and scheme for what to-morrow brings;
We sleep, perchance, and never wake again,
Nor taste life's joys, or suffer sorrow's stings.
Will the soul soar, or will it sink below?
How can we know.

You must have Faith!" - How can a mortal weak,
Pin faith on what he cannot comprehend?
We grope for light, - but all in vain we seek,
Oblivion seems poor mortal's truest friend.
Like bats at noonday, blindly on we go,
For naught we know.

Yet, why should we repine? Could we but see
Our lifelong journey with its ups and downs!
Ambition, hope and longings all would flee,
Indifferent alike to smiles and frowns.
'Tis better as it is. It must be so.
We ne'er can know.

John Hartley

Do something strange today.

**Make some plan today for what you will do to
create a new venture in your life...whatever it is.**

Go somewhere today that you rarely if ever go.

Talk to some stranger today and see what you learn.

Think of someone you know who is truly adventurous...in a good sense.

See and enjoy the adventure in your life...or create one!

A VERY COMMON BELIEF IS THAT IN OUR MECHANICAL UNIVERSE WE ALONE POSSESS CONSCIOUSNESS AND THE WHEREWITHAL TO MOULD THE WORLD ACCORDING TO OUR DESIGN.

MAYBE IT IS NOT SO.

Maybe, in designing our world we do so in respect for the greater design that is at work in the universe and in our own hearts.

We have a unique part to play in helping the universe reach its rich fulfilment and in doing so we listen to what the universe is saying to us both now and in other times and traditions.

Why not act and live today as if THIS version is true.

It will enrich everything you do and transform your day. And….as a matter of fact…it IS true.

LISTEN TO

CHOOSE YOUR OWN ADVENTURE
BY
GOLDFISH

SCAN WITH SMARTPHONE

235

SIMBA'S
TIP FOR TODAY

... from his latest book:
On the Loose in a Dog's World

No matter how far you stray, there is always a home to come back to.

YOUR BRAIN
TEASER FOR TODAY

MAN: HOW MANY BIRDS AND HOW MANY BEASTS DO YOU HAVE IN YOUR ZOO?

ZOOKEEPER: THERE ARE 30 HEADS AND 100 FEET.

MAN: I CAN'T TELL FROM THAT.

ZOOKEEPER: OH YES, YOU CAN!

CAN YOU?

YOUR
MANAGEMENT
MESSAGE
FOR
TODAY
IS

MANAGING
TO BE
HUMAN

...DING BUSINESS ORGANISATIONS
...TH INTEGRITY AND EFFECTIVENESS

BRIAN F. SMYTH

Creativity and thinking and working in creative ways are not things we can just turn on and off. It is an attitude to life and to the world. It is about trying to live each day as creatively – in the full sense of that word, as already mentioned – as possible.

Doing this is the work of a lifetime and making this happen and making it part of our lives will not happen by default. One way that I find helpful is to try to make the most of each day and treat it as a gift. This needs to begin early. If you don't catch the day early on, you may find yourself in the middle of it...and lost in it. For that reason it is a good practice to get the day off to a positive start.

One way to do this is to use a process similar to one that author Anthony Robbins recommends. So, every morning when you wake up, instead of letting a flood of worries and anxieties or the morning radio good-mood assassination show take you over, why don't you decide what you think and take control of your brain.

See next page

YOU CAN DO THIS BY DELIBERATELY ASKING YOURSELF SOME QUESTIONS

What am I happy about in my life at present?
How does that make me feel?

What am I excited about in my life?
How does that make me feel?

What am I proud of in my life at the moment?
How does that make me feel?

What am I grateful for in my life at present?
How does that make me feel?

What am I committed to in my life at present?
How does that make me feel?

Who loves me and who do I love?
How does that make me feel?

END OF DAY

ANY NICE ADVENTURES TODAY...OR EVEN THOUGHT OF OR PLANNED?

REMEMBER TOMORROW IS AN OPPORTUNITY TO BEGIN OR GO AFTER NEW ONES.

SAY THANKS FOR ALL THE ADVENTURES IN YOUR LIFE, BIG AND SMALL.

DAY 24

He who knows that enough is enough will always have enough.

Lao Tzu

Today you will enjoy abundance and how plentiful life and everything is.

YOU first of all have to realise how abundant YOU are and feel the riches and richness in YOU.

Whatever your circumstances, think of how much you have around you compared to what you really or absolutely need to survive.

Feel yourself part of nature, and feel how immense and enormous you are.

Remember that there are only five links between you and anybody in the world? What a reach you have!

Think of how much is there for you in the world in every realm to be explored, known, enjoyed – books, music, cultures, foods, flowers, perfumes, people, etc ...

ABUNDANCE AND LETTING GO

The Guru sat in meditation on the riverbank when a disciple bent down to place two enormous pearls at his feet, a token of reverence and devotion. The Guru opened his eyes, lifted one of the pearls and held it so carelessly that it slipped out of his hand and rolled down the bank into the river.

The horrified disciple plunged in after it but, though he dived in again and again until late evening, he had no luck.

Finally, all wet and exhausted, he roused the Guru from his meditation:
"You saw where it fell. Show me the spot so I can get it back for you."

The Guru lifted the other pearl, threw it into the river and said, "Right there!"

YOU WILL HAVE VERY RICH COMPANY TODAY AS YOU ENJOY HOW PLENTIFUL YOUR WORLD AND THE WHOLE WORLD IS FROM PEOPLE WHO JOINED US AND THE WORLD ON THIS DAY AND GREATLY ENRICHED IT AND ALL OF US.

JORGE LUIS BORGES

GILBERT BECAUD

DUSTIN HOFFMAN

H. DE TOULOUSE LAUTREC

ROGER FEDERER

SCOTT JOPLIN

STEPHEN FRY

IGNATIUS OF LOYOLA

SIR ARTHUR GUINNESS

BILLY CONNOLLY

HOW COULD YOU NOT HAVE A DAY OF PLENTY IN THE COMPANY OF SOME OF THESE WHO ADDED SO MUCH RICHNESS TO OUR WORLD. CHOOSE JUST ONE OR TWO FOR TODAY, FOR THIS MONTH.

WHAT QUALITIES DO THEY HAVE THAT YOU WOULD LIKE TO HAVE?
WHAT QUALITIES DO YOU HAVE THAT YOU ARE EITHER NOT SUFFICIENTLY AWARE OF OR ARE NOT PUTTING TO ENOUGH GOOD USE?
HOW CAN YOU PRACTISE AND LIVE THESE TODAY?

IF WE HAD BUT A DAY

WE should fill the hours with the sweetest things,
If we had but a day;
We should drink alone at the purest springs
In our upward way;

We should love with a lifetime's love in an hour,
If the hours were few;
We should rest, not for dreams, but for fresher power
To be and to do.

We should guide our wayward or wearied wills
By the clearest light;
We should keep our eyes on the heavenly hills,
If they lay in sight;

We should trample the pride and the discontent
Beneath our feet;
We should take whatever a good God sent,
With a trust complete.

We should waste no moments in weak regret,
If the day were but one;
If what we remember and what we forget
Went out with the sun;

We should be from our clamorous selves set free,
To work or to pray,
And to be what the Father would have us be,
If we had but a day.

Mary Lowe Dickinson

Find a leaf today and look at it...in detail.

Then compare it to another from the same tree or source.

Notice the differences.

On just one tree there are over 250,000 leaves and not ONE of them the same as another.

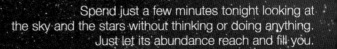

Spend just a few minutes tonight looking at the sky and the stars without thinking or doing anything. Just let its abundance reach and fill you.

Spend 20 seconds in silence and experience the calm and abundance all around you.

You have three times that available in just one minute.

Even if you lived for only one hour, you would have experienced enormous abundance.

A FEW CENTURIES AGO THE NOTION DEVELOPED AND GOT ACCEPTED BY EVERYONE THAT FOR THE RELIGIOUS, TO BE SACRED IS TO BE OTHERWORLDLY; THE SOUL IS SEPARATE FROM THE BODY, AND GOD LIVES HIGH ABOVE THE EARTH.

YES, BUT THIS WAS A TRAGEDY for the religious and for the world.

God lives in everything and everything reflects and represents the presence of God.

God can be found and is to be found in everything even in a grain of sand as William Blake said.

Where is the sacred in your daily life?

Find three examples of the truly sacred in what you do and meet today.

LISTEN TO

IMAGINE
BY
JOHN LENNON

SCAN WITH SMARTPHONE

SIMBA'S
TIP FOR TODAY

... from Volume 3 of: *No limits in a Dog's World*

There is never a shortage of sticks to run after and bring back

YOUR BRAIN TEASER FOR TODAY

You are the executor for the will of a poor but fair farmer who died leaving 17 cows.

His will specified that the cows be divided among his three sons as follows:

Half to the oldest son
One third to the second son
One ninth to the youngest son.

WHAT WILL YOU DO?

YOUR MANAGEMENT MESSAGE FOR TODAY IS

Controls and fear of mistakes and things going wrong, while understandable and healthy, can dominate in organisations and create an atmosphere of fear and caution and negativity.

Equally strong positive mechanisms need to be introduced that celebrate successes, that pursue opportunities, that recognise achievements, that look for new possibilities, and that set high goals and targets. Above all, organisations need people of hope and positive and visionary leaders.

New ideas will not progress unless this kind of positive environment exists and creating such an environment is a key role for a leader. Be positive.

DING BUSINESS ORGANISATIONS
TH INTEGRITY AND EFFECTIVENESS

MANAGING TO BE HUMAN

BRIAN F. SMYTH

END OF DAY

REMEMBER THE LEAVES, REMEMBER THE STARS, REMEMBER THE SECONDS. WHAT
A FULL AND PLENTIFUL DAY YOU HAVE HAD.

DID YOU MAKE THE MOST OF IT?

DON'T WORRY, ANOTHER ONE ARRIVES TOMORROW.

DAY 25

Don't try to make life a mathematical problem with yourself in the centre and everything coming out equal.

When you are good, bad things can still happen. And if you are bad, you can still be lucky.

Barbara Kingslover

?!?

Today you will dance with serendipity, chance, luck, fortune.

It will not be a nervous dance but a very relaxed and graceful one.

You will smile and trust your partner who has been with you all your life.

Often you did not even know that she was there and you believed you were on your own.

But, when you look back at your life and see where you are today, you will see the wonderful and magical partner who was with you all along.

No major fortuitous events may happen to you today but this does not mean that your partner, – serendipity, chance etc.– has gone away or even gone asleep.

Enjoy it all and take her/him/it in your arms or rest in her/his/its arms.

A LITTLE stream had lost its way
　Amid the grass and fern;
A passing stranger scooped a well,
　Where weary men might turn;
He walled it in and hung with care
　A ladle at the brink;
He thought not of the deed he did,
　But judged that all might drink.
He passed again, and lo! the well,
　By summer never dried,
Had cooled ten thousand parching tongues,
　And saved a life beside.

A nameless man, amid a crowd
　That thronged the daily mart,
Let fall a word of hope and love,
　Unstudied, from the heart;
A whisper on the tumult thrown,
　A transitory breath—
It raised a brother from the dust,
　It saved a soul from death.
O germ! O fount! O word of love!
　O thought at random cast!
Ye were but little at the first,
　But mighty at the last.

Charles Mackay

PERSPECTIVES CAN BE MAGIC!

An English man migrated to the United States and became an American citizen.

When he went back to England for a vacation one of his relatives reprimanded him for changing his citizenship.

"What did you gain by becoming an American citizen?" She asked him.

"Well, for one thing. I won the American Revolution"

Said the river to the seeker: "Does one really have to worry about enlightenment? I find that no matter which way I turn, I am homeward bound."

IN CASE YOU SHOULD FORGET THE WONDERFUL PARTNER YOU HAVE WITH YOU, THERE ARE SOME SPECIAL PEOPLE BORN ON THIS VERY DATE WHO WANT TO KEEP REMINDING YOU THAT YOU ARE NOT ALONE AT ALL.

LEONARD BERNSTEIN

PABLO PICASSO

SEAN CONNERY

AL PACINO

CLAUDIA SCHIFFER

JOE DIMAAGGIO

RONNIE BARKER

PETER ILYICH TCHAIKOVSKY

GEORGES BIZET

POPE JOHN 23RD

WHICH TWO OF THESE WOULD YOU LIKE BY YOUR SIDE TODAY TO KEEP YOU AWAKE AND AWARE OF THE CHANCE THAT IS ALWAYS AT PLAY IN YOUR LIFE AND IN THE WORLD?

WHAT QUALITIES DO THEY HAVE THAT YOU WOULD LIKE TO HAVE?
WHAT QUALITIES DO YOU HAVE THAT YOU ARE EITHER NOT SUFFICIENTLY AWARE OF OR ARE NOT PUTTING TO ENOUGH GOOD USE?
HOW CAN YOU PRACTISE AND LIVE THESE TODAY?

My life is filled with love, yes, true love, I do decree
I give myself to love, like an ever present devotee
Every hug and kiss I treasure and accept with glee
I have it all you see, luck just seems to follow me

I don't hobble through life as though I am an amputee
No shackles can hold me back, I am not a detainee
Obstacle are faced head on, I never run away like an escapee
I have it all you see, luck just seems to follow me

Life is not a bed of roses, and at times it's like a judas tree
Life is beset by problems, but from them I never flee
Every problem is welcomed, as an opportunity
I have it all you see, luck just seems to follow me

In life nothing is for sure, there is no guarantee
My life was spent perfecting what is now a 'life degree'
I am so blessed that you simply must agree
I have it all. You see, luck just seems to follow me

Michael Sage

Luck Follows Me

I have it all - some say I got it all for free
Everything I do, turns into a leafy golden tree
The waters part for me, even in a turbulent sea
I have it all you see, luck just seems to follow me

My kids are healthy, happy and totally free
My wife - caring, special and oh so lovely
My life is full of special souls, they're my family
I have it all you see, luck just seems to follow me

Find one example today of serendipity or chance in your life.

It may or may not have happened today.

Place a bet, buy a lottery ticket, do something just for the fun.

See who pops into your head today out of the blue and, whoever it is, make contact with them.

Who knows what may happen!

Do something today that you want to do and that is of some importance even if you are not hopeful about the chances of it working.

Surprise someone and expect some surprise today.

THE MORE POWERFUL WE ARE, THE BETTER OFF WE ARE IN THIS INDIFFERENT OR HOSTILE UNIVERSE AND THE MORE COMFORTABLE AND SECURE.

NO, we are the products, children, of our universe, and we will be better off the more we respect and honour our mother universe in relationships of gratitude, trust and love.

We do not need to fight, or compete or dominate others. We are all brothers and sisters, children of the one mother and we only have to really believe this for it to be absolutely true.

See if you can find examples today of how your power and resources could be actually causing you discomfort and insecurity.

Look at those around you today as your real brothers and sisters even if they too are blind to it...still.

LISTEN TO

LUCK
BY
AMERICAN AUTHORS

SCAN WITH SMARTPHONE

SIMBA'S
TIP FOR TODAY

... from his last book: *It's Still a Dog's Life*

You never know what you will find when you go digging or exploring

YOUR BRAIN
TEASER FOR TODAY

Lucky Sally

Sally was on her way home from her driving test and was still feeling very nervous even though she had passed the test.

She was not fully concentrating on where she was going and she went straight over a zebra crossing. Then she went the wrong way up a one-way street.

A policeman saw it all but did absolutely nothing.

Why? Was Sally just lucky?

YOUR
MANAGEMENT
MESSAGE
FOR
TODAY
IS

As a manager you can be a kind of alchemist – turning the base metal of existing reality into golden opportunities and rich outcomes.

Our own belief systems and our belief in people and in life are essential for achieving this.

If we really believe in our people, they will believe in themselves. If we really believe in the wealth of possibilities around us in every moment, others will see them too.

We can structure and carry out our work to ensure that this belief in people and in the possibilities in life and in every situation are alive, visible and touch people.

...DING BUSINESS ORGANISATIONS
...TH INTEGRITY AND EFFECTIVENESS

MANAGING
TO BE
HUMAN

BRIAN F. SMYTH

END OF DAY

I HOPE YOU CAME ACROSS AT LEAST ONE EXPERIENCE OF LUCK OR CHANCE TODAY.

IF NOT, WHO KNOWS WHAT MAY HAPPEN AT SOME TIME IN THE FUTURE AND YOU WILL LOOK BACK ON TODAY AND ONLY THEN RECOGNISE WHAT HAPPENED.

YOU KNOW YOU ARE NOT IN CONTROL OF EVERYTHING BUT YOU ARE IN GOOD HANDS – THE HANDS OF SERENDIPITY AND CHANCE.

DAY 26

It is the quality of compassionate presence and silence that enables us to hear our own words as well as those of others.

Donagh O Shea

Today you will pay attention to words and to what you say and to what you hear.

Words are incredibly unreliable, open to misinterpretation and misunderstanding and yet they are all we have to communicate directly.

Pay attention today to what you say, why you say it and to how you say it.

Be aware of the effect of your words on others.

Be equally aware of the effects others' words have on you and conscious of what you are doing to what was said through your interpretation, 'tranlsation', distortion etc.

Have fun today with all those words that are going to get said today and with what they reveal and hide.

HEARING FEEDBACK

When the Irish playwright **Oscar Wilde** arrived at his London club late at night after witnessing the first presentation of a play that had been a complete failure, someone asked, "How did your play go tonight?"

"Oh," said Wilde, "the play was a great success.

The audience was a failure."

IN CASE THIS IS AN ONEROUS OR NEBULOUS TASK FOR YOU,
YOU HAVE VERY GOOD COMPANIONS WHO HEARD THEIR FIRST WORDS ON THIS DATE!

MOTHER TERESA

T. S. ELIIOT

ROBERTSON DAVIES

MARTIN HEIDEGGER

GUILLAUME APOLINAIRE

MARTY ROBBINS

LEVI SSTRAUSS

OLIVIA NEWTON JOHN

FRANCIS OF ASSISSI

FATS DOMINO

QUITE A CHOICE. YOU CAN LISTEN TO TWO OF THESE OR JUST BE IN SILENCE WITH
THEM SO YOU CAN HEAR WORDS SPOKEN AND WORDS THOUGHT OR FELT.

WHAT QUALITIES DO THEY HAVE THAT YOU WOULD LIKE TO HAVE?
WHAT QUALITIES DO YOU HAVE THAT YOU ARE EITHER NOT SUFFICIENTLY AWARE OF OR ARE NOT
PUTTING TO ENOUGH GOOD USE?
HOW CAN YOU PRACTISE AND LIVE THESE TODAY?

Three Gates

If you are tempted to reveal
A tale to you someone has told
About another, make it pass,
Before you speak, three gates of gold.
These narrow gates: First, "Is it true?"
Then, "Is it needful?" In your mind
Give truthful answer.

And the next
Is last and narrowest, "Is it kind?"
And if to reach your lips at last
It passes through these gateways three,
Then you may tell the tale, nor fear
What the result of speech may be.

Arabian proverb.

TIS A STRANGE MYSTERY, THE POWER OF WORDS!
LIFE IS IN THEM, AND DEATH. A WORD CAN SEND
THE CRIMSON COLOUR HURRYING TO THE CHEEK,
HURRYING WITH MANY MEANINGS; OR CAN TURN
THE CURRENT COLD AND DEADLY TO THE HEART.
ANGER AND FEAR ARE IN THEM; GRIEF AND JOY
ARE ON THEIR SOUND; YET SLIGHT,
IMPALPABLE:--
A WORD IS BUT A BREATH OF PASSING AIR.

LETITIA ELIZABETH LANDON

Read a poem today...maybe your favourite or if not any poem...any good one.

Listen to the words beyond the actual meaning.

Read the first few lines of St. John's Gospel in the Bible and think what he could have meant.

SAY something today to someone that you would not normally say.

Listen to what people are saying today and to their every word and to what they are trying to say behind the words.

THERE ARE TIMES WHEN WE SEE LOTS OF ENEMIES AROUND US, NOT NECESSARILY EVIL OR BAD PEOPLE BUT PEOPLE WE NEED TO WATCH AND WE NEED TO GET THEM BEFORE THEY GET US. WE CAN FEEL MISTRUSTFUL AND AFRAID AND VERY CAUTIOUS.

NO, while there is no doubt that we are not surrounded by gentle, caring angels we must also remember that every person we encounter and every experience we have, mirrors something in ourselves.

If we did not know greed or ambition in ourselves, we could never spot it in others.

"If you spot it, you've got it."

Use today as an opportunity to see yourself in the faults and flaws you see in others as if they were holding a mirror up to you.

Humbling but rewarding.

LISTEN TO

WORDS
BY
BEE GEES

SCAN WITH SMARTPHONE

SIMBA'S
TIP FOR TODAY

… from his book: *My Life as a Dog*

I find, it's the tone
or the sound that
matters more
than the words

YOUR BRAIN
TEASER FOR TODAY

A friend came to stay recently.
When I knocked on her door the
next morning I asked her a question.

She said 'Yes'.

I knew she was lying!

WHAT WAS MY QUESTION?

YOUR
MANAGEMENT
MESSAGE
FOR
TODAY
IS

The principle is that very often we react to some behaviour or feature in another person which affects us negatively. In many cases the person is not having nearly the same effect on other people as they are having on us.

We can explain this by believing that we are more sensitive or more perceptive than others, but we don't really believe this to be so in all cases. For example, I can regard a colleague in a meeting as dominant because I want to have my say and I lack the confidence to participate in the conversation.

What is going on for me is that my own insecurity or lack of confidence is being triggered and I am feeling badly. I label a feeling of insecurity on my part as 'dominating' in the other person.

We need to listen and be aware of what the other person is saying or doing, and listen and be equally aware of what we are saying and doing to ourselves.

LEADING BUSINESS ORGANISATIONS
WITH INTEGRITY AND EFFECTIVENESS

MANAGING
TO BE
HUMAN

BRIAN F. SMYTH

END OF DAY

HOPE YOUR HEAD IS BUZZING WITH ALL THE WORDS YOU SAID AND HEARD AND THOUGHT TODAY.

THINK OF ONE WORD THAT SUMMARISES YOUR DAY…WHATEVER IT IS.

STAY WITH IT FOR A WHILE…IT'S REAL, REALITY AND SO IS GOOD.

SAY ONE WORD TO YOURSELF ABOUT WHAT YOU LOVE MOST ABOUT YOURSELF AND ABOUT LIFE.

DAY 27

One person with passion is worth 40 people merely interested.

E. M. Forster

Today's theme is about the exciting and about passion.

Now, you may not feel a bit like this and the day may not turn out a bit exciting and you may feel devoid of passion. That does not matter.

You can still admire it and celebrate it in life or in others, and a glorious sunset does not depend on how you feel and even exists without you.

You will see or meet or hear about at least five people who are truly passionate today.

You will find at least three things today to be excited about, even if you don't actually feel excited. Even when it is night and dark you still believe in day and light, so even if you are dull or down, you can still believe in excitement and passion.

IF YOU ARE HAVING TROUBLE FINDING SOURCES OR EXAMPLES OF EXCITEMENT OR PASSION WE HAVE A FEW PEOPLE TO HELP YOU, PEOPLE WHO FIRST BROUGHT SOME EXCITEMENT AND PASSION ON THIS DAY WHEN THEY WERE BORN:

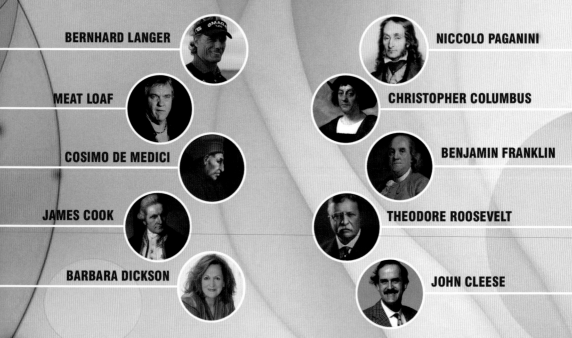

BERNHARD LANGER

NICCOLO PAGANINI

MEAT LOAF

CHRISTOPHER COLUMBUS

COSIMO DE MEDICI

BENJAMIN FRANKLIN

JAMES COOK

THEODORE ROOSEVELT

BARBARA DICKSON

JOHN CLEESE

CHOOSE ONE OR TWO OF THESE TO ACCOMPANY YOU ON THIS DAY OF PASSION AND EXCITEMENT.

WHAT QUALITIES DO THEY HAVE THAT YOU WOULD LIKE TO HAVE?
WHAT QUALITIES DO YOU HAVE THAT YOU ARE EITHER NOT SUFFICIENTLY AWARE OF OR ARE NOT PUTTING TO ENOUGH GOOD USE?
HOW CAN YOU PRACTISE AND LIVE THESE TODAY?

PASSION

I rock and roll with passion
I talk out my soul with a passion
I eat good food with passion
I defeat bad mood with a passion
I sleep well with passion
I weep hell with a passion
I dream endlessly with passion
I gleam ceaselessly with a passion
I aim for money with passion
I do the same for honey with a passion
I listen carefully with passion
I glisten dutifully with a passion
I search for fame with passion
I research to blame with a passion
I walk everyday with passion
I talk and play with a passion
I embrace life with passion

I face nightlife with a passion
I laugh out with passion
I chaffe about with a passion
I cook with others with passion
I look at mothers with a passion
I touch gently with passion
I clutch tightly with a passion
I work hard with a passion
I rock mad with a passion
I gear up goals with passion
I stir up roles with a passion
I make friends with passion
I take weekends with a passion
I love kissing with passion
I love teasing with a passion
I make love with passion
I take from above with a passion

If push comes to shove
Label me old fashioned
For these are things I caption
In life with all my passion

SYLVIA CHIDI

271

Today do at least one exciting thing…even if you don't feel like it.

Identify two or three people you know who are passionate about what they do.

Carry out some ordinary task you do today with real passion

Talk to someone who you believe lives an exciting life.

What is one thing you are or could be passionate about?

Recall some truly exciting moment or experience in your life.

WHERE TO FIND MOTIVATION

An old pilgrim was making his way to the Himalayan mountains in the bitter cold of winter when it began to rain.

An innkeeper said to him, "How will you ever get there in this kind of weather, my good man?"

The old man answered cheerfully, "My heart got there first, so it's easy for the rest of me to follow."

Where is YOUR heart set?

OK THEN! SO, IF THE BLIND, RUTHLESS PURSUIT OF SELF-INTEREST IS ANTISOCIAL, IT IS SURELY IMPORTANT, THEN, TO OVERCOME OUR BIOLOGICAL PROGRAMMING AND PURSUE "HIGHER THINGS."

NO. NOT REALLY.

We are spiritual through and through as is everything in our surroundings and universe.

The more we plunge ourselves into, immerse ourselves in, truly embrace the real, the earth, the world, people, the more we will experience the spirit that is at work in everything.

We do not need to remove or distance ourselves from the world, life or people but to spot the spirit at work in them and in everything, however hidden it may sometimes be.

LISTEN TO
PASSION
BY
DANNY WRIGHT

SCAN WITH SMARTPHONE

... from his philosophical work:
To Be or not to Be in a Dog's World

There is never a day without some adventure in it if you look or wait for it

YOUR BRAIN
TEASER FOR TODAY

Mr. Smith eats two eggs every day.

He never buys any eggs, nobody gives him eggs, he doesn't steal them from anyone and he doesn't keep hens.

WHERE DOES HE GET HIS EGGS FROM?

YOUR
MANAGEMENT
MESSAGE
FOR
TODAY
IS

There are so many visions hanging on walls full of nice words and empty of any passion. Your vision has to be you, to represent you and your values.

If not, people will sense or smell it from you.

It has to be something that you would do a lot to achieve, that touches your deepest desires and that is in line with your dreams, old and new. It should score well on all of the three points of the Goals Triangle, as applying to the company or your part in it:

- *What is it that is really NEEDED?*
- *What do you really LIKE and WANT?*
- *What are your CAPABILITIES or COMPETENCIES?*

DING BUSINESS ORGANISATIONS
TH INTEGRITY AND EFFECTIVENESS

MANAGING
TO BE
HUMAN

BRIAN F. SMYTH

END OF DAY

WHAT WAS THE MOST EXCITING THING YOU DID TODAY?

ANY ADVENTURES? EVEN THOUGHT OF?

WHAT OPPORTUNITIES FOR RISK AND FUN DID YOU MISS.
(DON'T WORRY, THERE IS ALWAYS TOMORROW!)

DAY 28

Our greatest joy requires that we remember our deepest loss.

Roger S. Gottlieb

- TODAY'S THEME IS SADNESS, LOSS, EVEN DEATH!

- NOW, LIKE OTHER DAYS YOU MAY NOT BE IN THIS MOOD AT ALL, AND GREAT IF YOU ARE NOT.

- HOWEVER, IT IS STILL A THEME OR TOPIC WORTH VISITING BECAUSE IT IS REAL AND BECAUSE IT IS THE REVERSE SIDE OF JOY, LIFE ETC. AND SO PART OF THEM IN SOME SENSE.

- SO, DON'T BE AFRAID TO HAVE THESE PRESENT TO YOU TODAY. THEY WON'T UPSET YOUR DAY AT ALL AND VISITING THEM WILL GIVE YOU AN EVEN DEEPER HAPPINESS AND JOY.

- A FRIEND SAID TO ME ONCE: "IT'LL BE A SAD DAY WHEN WE CAN'T CRY".

- I TAKE IT YOU DO KNOW WHAT THESE MOMENTS OR FEELINGS MEAN AND YOU HAVE EXPERIENCED THEM IN DIFFERENT WAYS AT SOME STAGE IN YOUR LIFE, EITHER A LONG TIME AGO OR MORE RECENTLY. OR YOU MAY BE EXPERIENCING SOME VERSION OF THEM RIGHT NOW IN YOUR LIFE.

- WHEN YOU RECALL THEM DURING THE DAY DON'T LET THEM DRAG YOU DOWN AND DON'T SPEND TIME GOING OVER AND OVER THEM OR TRYING TO RESOLVE THEM. JUST BE PRESENT TO THEM AND HAVE THEM PRESENT TO YOU, AND LIVE YOUR DAY IN HAPPINESS AND WELL-BEING IN SPITE OF THEM, OR EVEN THROUGH THEM. YOU CAN. AND YOUR DAY AND YOUR HAPPINESS WILL HAVE AN EVEN GREATER DEPTH TO THEM.

"Sorrow prepares you for joy.
It violently sweeps everything out of your house,
so that new joy can find space to enter.
It shakes the yellow leaves from the bough of your heart,
so that fresh, green leaves can grow in their place.
It pulls up the rotten roots, so that new roots hidden beneath have room to grow.
Whatever sorrow shakes from your heart, far better things will take their place."

Rumi

LOSS -THE FINAL SOLUTION
JUNE 22ND 1941 TO MAY 8, 1945

"Thus for the overall total in my field of activities we have an average of 572,043 dead per month, 131, 410 dead per week, 18,722 dead per day, 782 dead per hour, and 13.04 dead per minute , every minute of every hour of every day of every week of every month of every year of the given period, which is, as you will recall, three years, 10 months, 16 days, 20 hours, and one minute.

Let those who smirk at that admittedly somewhat pedantic extra minute please consider that it is worth an additional 13.04 dead, on average, and imagine, if they can, 13 people from their circle of friends killed in one minute. "

Jonathan Littell *The Friendly Ones*

"When those dear to us were alive, they were with us when they were with us. When they are dead, they are with us, ALL THE TIME."

St John Chrysostom.

YOU WILL LIVE YOUR DAY OF SADNESS AND LOSS AND JOY IN GOOD COMPANY.
PEOPLE WHO KNEW IT AND LIVED THROUGH IT WHO WERE BORN ON THIS DATE.

CLAUDE DEBUSSY

ANDRE GIDE

ANDREA BOCELLI

RALPH FIENNES

HARPER LEE

CHICO MARX

FRANZ LISZT

ARTHUR SCHOPENHAUER

LINUS PAULING

TED KENNEDY

OK? MANY OF THESE HAVE OVERCOME ALL KINDS OF SETBACKS AND DONE GREAT THINGS.
CHOOSE ONE OR TWO TO BE WITH YOU TODAY AS YOU DO YOUR GREAT THINGS.

WHAT QUALITIES DO THEY HAVE THAT YOU WOULD LIKE TO HAVE?
WHAT QUALITIES DO YOU HAVE THAT YOU ARE EITHER NOT SUFFICIENTLY AWARE OF OR ARE NOT
PUTTING TO ENOUGH GOOD USE?
HOW CAN YOU PRACTISE AND LIVE THESE TODAY?

Watch the film

The Last Days of Sophie Scholl

when you can!

IT CAN FEEL, AT TIMES, THAT WE MUST EXERCISE AS MUCH CONTROL AS POSSIBLE TO PROTECT OURSELVES AGAINST A HOSTILE UNIVERSE OF COMPETING INDIVIDUALS AND IMPERSONAL FORCES. IT'S THE NAME OF THE GAME.

MAYBE.

Maybe there is really a very different game. A game in which the universe is friendly and everything in it wants to cooperate for the welfare of the whole in loving and joyful harmony.

The truth of this is only lost when we fail to understand and to live it.

Can you play this game today?
The game of cooperation and understanding?

Do so and it will be a world of cooperation and understanding.

LISTEN TO

LADY WITH THE BRAID
BY
DORY PREVIN

SCAN WITH SMARTPHONE

- Spend a little time today thinking of, and perhaps, talking to dear people you have lost for whatever reason.

- What were the big losses in your life, even if they might seem small to others?

- Say thanks for being able to be as good as you are despite your losses.

- If you feel loss or sadness or pain, accept it and act and live through it.
  Don't deny it, accept it but do all you are doing really well through the pain.

- Think of someone who may be sad today and talk to them.

- Notice anyone around you who may be suffering behind their look or their behaviour and hug them metaphorically or really.

- Be ready and ready to be brave for the next bad news you receive whenever it is and whatever it is. You can handle it…well.

NO ONE EVER
told me that grief felt sore like fear

C.S. Lewis

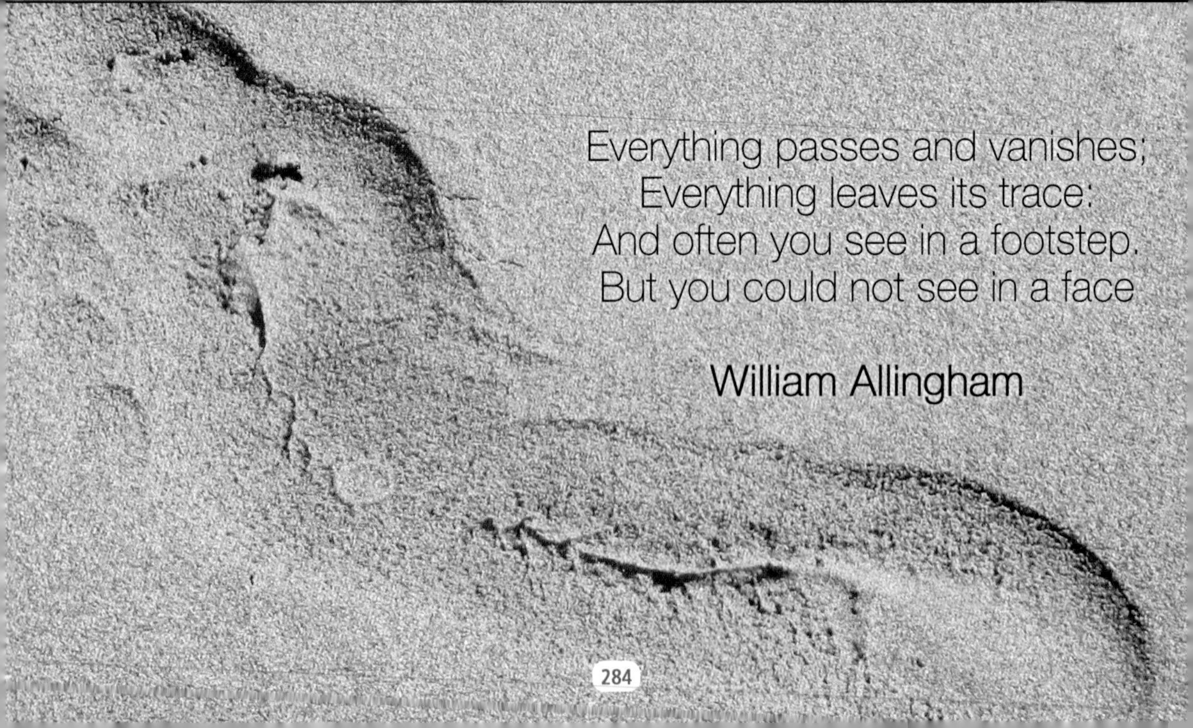

Everything passes and vanishes;
Everything leaves its trace:
And often you see in a footstep.
But you could not see in a face

William Allingham

SIMBA'S
TIP FOR TODAY

If someone gives you a kick,
don't pay any heed.
It will pass and they
may be having a bad day

YOUR BRAIN
TEASER FOR TODAY

Three men rent a room in an hotel.

The manager charges than €30 and gives them the key. After they're
gone to the room he realises that he has made a mistake.
The price of the room should be €25 and he has overcharged them €5.
He opens the till, takes out €5 in coins and calls the bellboy.

He gives the bellboy the five euro coins and tells him to give them to
the new guests. On the way to the room the bellboy realises that it is going
to be difficult to split five coins between three men so he decides to
keep life simple and gives them each €1, keeping €2 as a tip.

The men originally paid €10 and now get €1 euro back
so they have paid €9 Euro each for their room or a total of €27.

The bellboy has €2.

Where are the missing €2 gone?'

YOUR MANAGEMENT MESSAGE FOR TODAY IS

Be present to a problem or issue in all its complexity, mystery and difficulty without coming up with a thought-out answer or solution. As managers, we need to be clear and decisive and we feel we need to be so all the time. Not knowing what to do, uncertainty, being lost or stuck, being unsure are not states that sit easily with us. We like to get to some definite position or state of certainty.

This runs the risk of premature closure of the discussion without adequate investigation of an issue or situation. To get the contribution of our group or team we need to stay open and present problems, challenges and opportunities from a position of uncertainty, not knowing and being a bit lost or stuck. This may sound strange but life is full of problems that don't have any easy or quick solution.

It is going after a solution to these kinds of problems that will give the greatest gains. A huge gain is made just by deciding to go after a difficult problem or issue.

LEADING BUSINESS ORGANISATIONS WITH INTEGRITY AND EFFECTIVENESS

MANAGING TO BE HUMAN

BRIAN I. SMYTH

END OF DAY

BE GRATEFUL FOR WHAT YOU WERE ABLE TO DO TODAY.

TAKE SOMEONE'S SADNESS ON BOARD BUT CARRY IT WITH COURAGE AND EVEN JOY.

REMEMBER THAT NO MATTER HOW DARK OR LONG THE NIGHT IS, MORNING AND DAY
WILL COME FOR YOU AND FOR OTHERS.

DAY 29

Chaos was the law of nature;
Order was the dream of man.

Henry Adams

Today is all about chaos, confusion, being lost, not in control, the unknown!
Bet you are not looking forward to all that!

But why not? It is ok to be like that...not in control.

Already you have passed through many stages in your life where you
felt like this and you came through them fine.

For this, you have to trust – life, others and yourself.

Let yourself go and keep going even if the way ahead is no longer very clear.

Now, today may not be at all so confusing but you know what I am saying and it is
good to be in touch with it. There will be SOME aspect of your life that is like this.
You can practise it there.

Trust that there is an intelligence, a consciousness, a light at work
behind all the fog and mist and that all will be ok. You can do it.
You already have many times.

I have an idea that the only thing which makes it possible to regard this world we live in without disgust is the beauty which now and then men create out of the chaos. The pictures they paint, the music they compose, the books they write, and the lives they lead. Of all these the richest in beauty

is the beautiful life. That is the perfect work of art.

W. SOMERSET MAUGHAM

EASY TO GET CONFUSED!

A drunkard was walking down a street with blisters on both ears. A friend asked him what had happened to cause the blisters.

My wife left her iron on, so when the phone rang I picked up the iron by mistake."

"Yes, but what about the other ear?"

"The damn fool called back!"

TO GUIDE YOU THROUGH THE CHAOS AND THE CONFUSION TODAY, HOWEVER PRESENT IT MAY BE IN YOUR LIFE OR IN SOME PART OF YOUR LIFE, YOU HAVE SOME GREAT COMPANIONS WHO BEGAN THEIR CHAOTIC AND BEAUTIFUL LIVES ON THIS DATE.

INGRID BERGMAN

CARAVAGGIO

BOB BEAMON

HORATIO NELSON

MICHAEL JACKSON

HIROHITO

POMPEY THE GREAT

JERRY LEE LEWIS

MIGUEL DE CERVANTES

ANDRE AGASSI.

SURE YOU WILL FIND ONE OR TWO THERE TO INSPIRE YOU TO TRUST AND KEEP GOING BELIEVING IT WILL ALL BE FINE AND EVEN GREAT!

WHAT QUALITIES DO THEY HAVE THAT YOU WOULD LIKE TO HAVE?
WHAT QUALITIES DO YOU HAVE THAT YOU ARE EITHER NOT SUFFICIENTLY AWARE OF OR ARE NOT PUTTING TO ENOUGH GOOD USE?
HOW CAN YOU PRACTISE AND LIVE THESE TODAY?

Reflect on those moments in your life where you felt lost but kept going and all turned out fine … and maybe even better.

Where is there lack of clarity in your life right now?

Can you embrace it?
If you can, go for a walk today … in the country or in the city… without any plan and enjoy the vagueness and lostness of it.

Think of some area in your life now that you are concerned about and see if you can let go and trust life.

Talk to someone today without any idea what you are going to say or what the conversation is about and let it go ···and see what happens. Just trust the life in the dialogue.

Trust yourself. Take a gamble on someone about whom you are not really or fully confident and enjoy the risk.

THE CATERPILLAR

Under this loop of honeysuckle,
A creeping, coloured caterpillar,
I gnaw the fresh green hawthorn spray,
I nibble it leaf by leaf away.

Down beneath grow dandelions,
Daisies, old-man's-looking-glasses;
Rooks flap croaking across the lane.
I eat and swallow and eat again.

Here come raindrops helter-skelter;
I munch and nibble unregarding:
Hawthorn leaves are juicy and firm.
I'll mind my business: I'm a good worm.

When I'm old, tired, melancholy,
I'll build a leaf-green mausoleum
Close by, here on this lovely spray,
And die and dream the ages away.

Some say worms win resurrection,
With white wings beating flitter-flutter,
But wings or a sound sleep, why should I care?
Either way I'll miss my share.

Under this loop of honeysuckle,
A hungry, hairy caterpillar,
I crawl on my high and swinging seat,
And eat, eat, eat—as one ought to eat.

Robert Graves

THERE ARE TIMES WHEN WE BELIEVE THAT AT THE VERY FOUNDATION OF OUR NATURE, OUR MOTIVATIONS, AND OUR DESIRES, IS WHAT CAN ONLY BE CALLED EVIL. THAT THERE IS A RUTHLESS MAXIMISER OF SELF INTEREST AND THAT WE ARE ALL LIKE THAT TO SOME EXTENT.

YES, WE CAN BELIEVE THAT.

But our beliefs have power.

It also makes sense to believe that really evil is a mistake, an illusion, a ghost that people believe in and then act out of.

The good is what is true, real and full of power.

The good is the truth of what we are and what our universe is. Live this truth today and the ghosts will disappear.

But you have to DO it.

LISTEN TO

THE FUTURE
BY
LEONARD COHEN

SCAN WITH SMARTPHONE

293

SIMBA'S
TIP FOR TODAY

... from his book:
Helping the Blind – Part of a Dog's life

You are never really lost.
Just somewhere else

YOUR BRAIN
TEASER FOR TODAY

You are driving a bus.
Four people get on, three people get off,
then eight people get on and teen
people get off, then six people get on
and two more people get off.

What colour are the bus driver's eyes

"I searched for God among the Christians and on the Cross and therein I found Him not. I went into the ancient temples of idolatry; no trace of Him was there.

I entered the mountain cave of Hira and then went as far as Qandhar but God I found not.

With set purpose I fared to the summit of Mount Caucasus and found there only 'anqa's habitation.

Then I directed my search to the Kaaba, the resort of old and young; God was not there even. Turning to philosophy I inquired about him from ibn Sina but found Him not within his range.

I fared then to the scene of the Prophet's experience of a great divine manifestation only a "two bow-lengths' distance from him" but God was not there even in that exalted court.

Finally, I looked into my own heart and there I saw Him; He was nowhere else."

Rumi

YOUR MANAGEMENT MESSAGE FOR TODAY IS

LEADING BUSINESS ORGANISATIONS WITH INTEGRITY AND EFFECTIVENESS

MANAGING TO BE HUMAN

BRIAN F. SMYTH

From Managing to be Human

(Creativity) comes from a deep place within us through which we are in contact with the world around us. When we block our thinking or rational mind and get to this deeper place, we get in touch with truth and wisdom. When this insight arrives we are at first unable to give expression to it. Then it gets expressed in some new form, perhaps a painting, book or song, which is the representation and expression of what we discovered in our conscious or subconscious state.

We give birth to something but it is not all of our doing. We are partners in it and for this we have to stop our minds to let our other partner – the universe – play its part.

This is not easy. It is not easy to let go of our thinking minds and spend time feeling lost and waiting for something to happen. We want to be always in control and it is uncomfortable not to have answers, not to know. The temptation is for the mind to satisfy this need for control by coming up with answers. The trouble is the answers may come early and may not be good enough or equal to the situation. Instead, we need to get into a state of quiet where we wait, a state of 'no mind' as Eckhart Tolle calls it.

END OF DAY

THINK OF ALL OR ANY MOMENTS DURING THE DAY (OR YOUR LIFE) WHEN YOU FELT LOST OR CONFUSED BUT STUCK WITH IT AND WENT THROUGH IT.

YOU ARE HERE...SO MANY THINGS COULD HAVE HAPPENED TO PREVENT YOU BEING HERE BUT EVERYTHING CONSPIRED BEAUTIFULLY TO LOOK AFTER YOU. TOMORROW WILL BE THE SAME AND THE DAY AFTERWARDS ALSO.

SOON YOU ARE GOING TO ENTRUST YOURSELF TO SLEEP AND HAND YOURSELF OVER TO YOUR UNCONSCIOUS WHICH WILL ALSO DO A GREAT JOB KEEPING EVERYTHING GOING PERFECTLY IN YOUR 'ABSENCE'.

DAY 30

*Everyone has his own specific vocation or mission in life;
everyone must carry out a concrete assignment
that demands fulfilment.*

*Therein he cannot be replaced,
nor can his life be repeated, thus,
everyone's task is unique as his
specific opportunity to implement it.*

Viktor E. Frankl

Today is about mission

You are probably wondering what this means!
It means your mission as an organization and your mission as an individual, as a person.

It might sound grandiose to talk of a personal mission but it is real and important.

The tiniest of insects have a part to play in the whole and they play it.
They have little choice but to do so.

You do have a choice and your part, your unique part is, of course, much more important than theirs.

Do you know what your part is? What is expected from you? The unique contribution you can make? The special contribution you want to make?

'Your playing small doesn't serve the world', Marianne Williamson says.

Where you are and what you are doing may not have been the result of a well-thought out plan but however or why ever you got to where you are today, you can play an important part and make a big contribution, your special contribution.

Today you will think a little about this and take yourself seriously…with a smile of course.

IN CASE THIS IS VAGUE OR EVEN DIFFICULT FOR YOU TO DO, WE HAVE SOME GREAT COMPANY FOR YOU IN THE PERSON OF 'MISSIONARIES' WHO BEGAN THEIR MISSION IN THE WORLD ON THIS DATE.

MARK TWAIN

JONATHAN SWIFT

MARY SHELLEY

CHRISTOPHER COLUMBUS

ANGELO DUNDEE

ELIE WIESEL

EZRA POUND

JOHNNY MATHIS

WARREN BUFFETT

DIEGO MARADONA

YOU CAN EASILY FIND ONE OR TWO PEOPLE TODAY TO HELP YOU FIND OR BE MORE AWARE OF YOUR TRUE MISSION. OK?

WHAT QUALITIES DO THEY HAVE THAT YOU WOULD LIKE TO HAVE?
WHAT QUALITIES DO YOU HAVE THAT YOU ARE EITHER NOT SUFFICIENTLY AWARE OF OR ARE NOT PUTTING TO ENOUGH GOOD USE?
HOW CAN YOU PRACTISE AND LIVE THESE TODAY?

ISN'T IT CLEAR. DESPITE THEIR SUPERFICIAL OPPOSITION, SCIENCE AND RELIGION HAVE AGREED: THE SACRED IS NOT OF THIS WORLD. LET THEM LIVE SIDE BY SIDE AS GOOD NEIGHBOURS WITH HIGH FENCES!

NO! There is a different version of what good neighbours mean and there is a different version of how science and religion relate.

Science, true science, and true religion do agree – the world is shot through and through with mystery and beauty to be endlessly explored and enjoyed.

It is all around you.

Why not live out this principle today and make the whole secular day a wonderful and sacred one.

LISTEN TO
HEY DREAMER
BY
JOHN SPILLANE

SCAN WITH SMARTPHONE

The time will come
when, with elation
you will greet yourself arriving
at your own door, in your own mirror
and each will smile at the other's welcome,

and say, sit here. Eat.
You will love again the stranger who was
your self.
Give wine. Give bread. Give back your heart
to itself, to the stranger who has loved you

all your life, whom you ignored
for another, who knows you by heart.
Take down the love letters from the
bookshelf,

the photographs, the desperate notes,
peel your own image from the mirror.
Sit. Feast on your life.

Derek Walcott

"Prisoner at the bar," said the Grand Inquisitor, "you are charged with encouraging people to break the laws, traditions and customs of our holy religion. How do you plead?"

"Guilty your Honour".

"And with frequenting the company of heretics, prostitutes, public sinners, the extortionist tax-collectors, the colonial conquerors of our nation – in short, the excommunicated. How do you plead?"

"Guilty, your Honour."

"Finally, you are charged with revising, correcting, calling into question the sacred tenets of our faith. How do you plead?"

"Guilty, your Honour."

"What is your name?"

"Jesus Christ, your Honour."

Find one situation, cause, person either in your life or remote from it about which you feel strongly and do something or begin something about it today.

In what you are doing in your life now, how could you find a richer, better and deeper meaning to it?

Find it! It is there.

What do you think your world requires from you, is asking of you?

What is one quality that you have that makes you special? Are you making the most of it and putting it to good use?

Find some need in your environment, work or social, and take responsibility for doing something about it.

SIMBA'S
TIP FOR TODAY

... from his Work: *Called to live a Dog's Life*

Ever see a dog going nowhere?

YOUR BRAIN
TEASER FOR TODAY

A visitor was surprised when visiting a pastor to see a book on his shelf with 'Go to Hell' on it.

Has the pastor changed his colours?

YOUR
MANAGEMENT
MESSAGE
FOR
TODAY
IS

From Managing to be Human

Spend time working on what the company or organisation is about, what it is trying to do, its purpose. If we can do this and do it well then this will give meaning to everything that gets done in the company. It will provide a raison d'être for instructions, plans and projects, as people will see how they fit with and contribute to the overall purpose of the organisation or company.

In other words, what I do and am expected and asked to do will make sense to me as I see how it fits with what the overall purpose of the organisation is. It will have meaning and I will be able to do it because it is meaningful and makes sense, not because someone has told me to do it.

People come to meetings with all kinds of notions and agendas in their heads. Some come to be with other people, some come to fight with other people, some come to complain and some come to defend themselves.

The fact of the matter is, a meeting means different things to different people. For that reason we need to make clear to everyone what the real purpose of the meeting is and what the objectives for it are. This means that at least all are in the same room for the same reason and so there will be a better chance of making progress and of the meeting being a success.

....

ADING BUSINESS ORGANISATIONS
ITH INTEGRITY AND EFFECTIVENESS

MANAGING
TO BE
HUMAN

BRIAN F. SMYTH

END OF DAY

ANYTHING YOU DID TODAY THAT YOU FEEL PLEASED ABOUT BECAUSE IT WAS REALLY YOU?

WHAT IS ONE THING THAT HAPPENED TODAY THAT MIGHT POINT YOU IN A GOOD DIRECTION FOR YOU?

ANY CLUE FROM TODAY OF WHERE YOU MIGHT BE MISSING OUT ON MAKING THE KIND OF CONTRIBUTION YOU CAN?

DAY 31

You only live once, but if you do it right, once is enough.

Mae West

SECOND BY SECOND:

The clock master was about to fix the pendulum of the clock when, to his surprise, he heard the pendulum speak.

"Please, sir, leave me alone," the pendulum pleaded. "It would be an act of kindness on your part. Think of the number of times I will have to tick day and night. So many times each minute, 60 minutes an hour, 24 hours a day, 365 days a year. For year upon year....Millions of ticks. I could never do it."

But the Master answered wisely, "Don't think of the future. Just do one tick at a time and you will enjoy every tick for the rest of your life."

And that's exactly what the pendulum decided to do. It is still ticking merrily away.

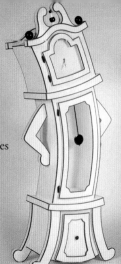

Today is all about Life and Hope. A day to enjoy and live.

And you can do this no matter what is happening today or in your life at present.

Life is everywhere, at work everywhere so find as many examples of life at work as you can today and enjoy and celebrate them.

Bring life to everything you do today and enliven everyone you come in contact with.

It is possible to be dead while still alive so you are going to ensure this does not happen in your presence.

Look at the life in children, your own or other children and feel their joy and hope.

See the life at work all around you in nature, in everything, the same life that you live or that lives you.

Make s   live every minute of this day and are alive in every single thing you do

YOU WILL NOT BE THE FIRST PERSON WHO REALLY LIVED THEIR LIVES AND EACH DAY.
OTHERS BEGAN DOING THAT ON THIS DATE

MARIA MONTESSORI

JAMES COBURN

ALAN JAY LERNER

WALT WHITMAN

JAN VERMEER

JOHN KEATS

TOM PAXTON

JOHN CANDY

JOHN DENVER

MARIO LANZA

FOUND SOME THERE WHO WILL HELP YOU TO STAY VERY ALIVE TODAY? HAVE ONE OR TWO OF THEM WITH
YOU TODAY HELPING YOU TO LIVE EVERY MOMENT AND TO NEVER LOSE HOPE, NO MATTER WHAT HAPPENS
BECAUSE THERE WILL ALWAYS BE LIFE AT WORK IN EVERYTHING AND IN EVERY MOMENT.

WHAT QUALITIES DO THEY HAVE THAT YOU WOULD LIKE TO HAVE?
WHAT QUALITIES DO YOU HAVE THAT YOU ARE EITHER NOT SUFFICIENTLY AWARE OF OR ARE NOT
PUTTING TO ENOUGH GOOD USE?
HOW CAN YOU PRACTISE AND LIVE THESE TODAY?

DO YOU EVER FEEL THAT, MUCH AS ONE WOULD LIKE TO TRUST PEOPLE AND THE WORLD AND LIVE IN A HEALTHY AND POSITIVE WAY, YOU ARE UP AGAINST IT BECAUSE THE WORLD IS NOT LIKE THAT AND YOU HAVE TO FIT IN WITH HOW THINGS ARE. NOR IS IT GOING TO CHANGE MUCH OR IN THE NEAR FUTURE. NOR CAN ONE PERSON DO MUCH ABOUT IT. SO, BAD AS YOU MAY FEEL ABOUT SOME THINGS AND MUCH AS YOU WOULD LIKE THEM TO BE DIFFERENT, YOU HAVE TO ACCEPT REALITY AND HAVE NO CHOICE BUT TO GO ALONG WITH THINGS.

MAYBE THE WORLD IS NOT LIKE THAT and maybe you have a lot more power to influence than you think?

Maybe things happen in magic or miraculous ways – all kinds of things. Maybe you have seen lots of these miracles in your own life already. What if you hold on to your dreams and values and refuse to give up on them. Do it and you will be surprised at what happens… and surprised at what you yourself do and can make happen.

The world needs this from you. We ALL need it from you.

LISTEN TO

WILL WE BE BRILLIANT OR WHAT
BY
JOHN SPILLANE

SCAN WITH SMARTPHONE

Every negative or 'no' you spot or hear today, check that it is not damaging or reducing life.

Walk, talk, do everything with life and energy. Communicate life and energy by everything you do.

Practise hoping but not expecting.

Think of three things you hope for in your life today and express that hope again but without being attached to what you hope for. That's up to life to give it or not!

Find someone who is down or going through a bad patch and be a source of hope for them today. Call them, talk to them, spend time with them.

Think of three good reasons —or people — for why you and we should be hopeful.

Take a walk somewhere there are trees or grass and see all the life that is always at work… for us…all the time.

... from his work: *Really live, live a Dog's Life*

As my friend, Snoopy, says, "Why was I born so lucky?"

YOUR BRAIN
TEASER FOR TODAY

While on safari in the wild jungles of Africa, professor Anna Gram woke one morning in her tent and felt something in the pocket of her pyjamas.

It had a head, a tail but no legs.

When Anna got up she could fee it move inside her pocket. However, Anna showed little concern and went about her morning activities.

Why was she not worried?

I like living.
I have sometimes been wildly,
despairingly, acutely miserable,
racked with sorrow,
but through it all I still know
that just to be alive is a grand thing

Agatha Christie

The most beautiful thing we can experience
is the mysterious.
It is the source of all true art and all science.
He to whom this emotion is a stranger,
who can no longer pause to wonder and stand rapt in awe,
is as good as dead: his eyes are closed.
Albert Einstein

The Invitation

It doesn't interest me what you do for a living.
I want to know what you ache for
and if you dare to dream of meeting your heart's longing.

It doesn't interest me how old you are.
I want to know if you will risk looking like a fool
for love
for your dream
for the adventure of being alive.

It doesn't interest me what planets are squaring your moon...
I want to know if you have touched the centre of your own sorrow
if you have been opened by life's betrayals
or have become shrivelled and closed
from fear of further pain.

I want to know if you can sit with pain
mine or your own
without moving to hide it
or fade it
or fix it.

I want to know if you can be with joy
mine or your own
if you can dance with wildness
and let the ecstasy fill you to the tips of your fingers and toes
without cautioning us
to be careful
to be realistic
to remember the limitations of being human.

It doesn't interest me if the story you are telling me
is true.
I want to know if you can
disappoint another
to be true to yourself.
If you can bear the accusation of betrayal
and not betray your own soul.
If you can be faithless
and therefore trustworthy.

I want to know if you can see Beauty
even when it is not pretty
every day.
And if you can source your own life
from its presence.

I want to know if you can live with failure
yours and mine
and still stand at the edge of the lake
and shout to the silver of the full moon,
"Yes."

It doesn't interest me
to know where you live or how much money you
have.
I want to know if you can get up
after the night of grief and despair
weary and bruised to the bone
and do what needs to be done
to feed the children.

It doesn't interest me who you know
or how you came to be here.
I want to know if you will stand
in the centre of the fire
with me
and not shrink back.

It doesn't interest me where or what or with whom
you have studied.
I want to know what sustains you

YOUR
MANAGEMENT
MESSAGE
FOR
TODAY
IS

A beggar sat on a box on a street asking passersby for some money.

As he saw a woman approach, he began his plea for some help.

The woman stopped and explained to the beggar that She had no money on her, but the beggar persisted, asking for just a little help. The woman asked the beggar what was in the box on which he was sitting.

'I don't know,' answered the beggar. 'I've never looked.' 'Why don't we have a look?' said the woman.

Between them they struggled with the box that hadn't been opened for a long time and was quite stuck.

When they finally got it open, they discovered that there was gold in the box.

You too are sitting on gold in terms of the enormous wealth in the people, in the resources and in the opportunities within your organisation and you are sitting on gold in terms of the enormous potential and richness that exist in you as a human being, which you may not have fully realised or appreciated.

ADING BUSINESS ORGANISATIONS
ITH INTEGRITY AND EFFECTIVENESS

MANAGING
TO BE
HUMAN

BRIAN F. SMYTH

DON'T STOP, KEEP PLAYING

A young mother who had encouraged her children to love piano music, took the most enthusiastic of them, the youngest, to Carnegie Hall for a Paderewski concert. She chose very expensive seats in the front row so the young lad could see the master pianist's fingers as they made marvellous music.

Just before the concert began, she spotted a friend a few rows back whom she hadn't seen for a long time and hurried to say hello to her. When she returned to her seat she was shocked to find her young son no longer there.

With that the curtain opened and she was even more shocked to see her son sitting at the piano merrily playing 'Twinkle, Twinkle Little Star'. Her shock turned to consternation on seeing Paderewski striding across the stage to his piano, taken over by the young lad. But, instead of removing the lad from the piano, he whispered something to him and began playing with the child with one arm either side of him. As they continued playing he repeated the whisper which it was subsequently discovered to be: "Don't stop, keep Playing."

They played on and on with Paderewski inventing and ad libbing and the child playing louder and louder, skipping some notes and improvising himself. They played for almost 12 minutes and then they both slid off the bench together and bowed as one. The audience went crazy, laughing, stomping their feet and applauding endlessly.

We need never worry over our paltry efforts to do great things and make the most of our beautiful lives. We are not alone. LIFE is with us always, cooperating with and enriching our efforts a hundred fold... and whispering: DON'T STOP, KEEP PLAYING.

(Courtesy Brendan Lovett)

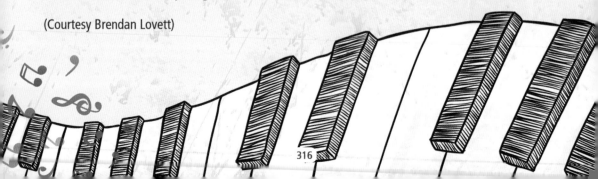

END OF DAY

THINK OF ONE OR TWO MOMENTS TODAY WHEN YOU FELT REALLY ALIVE, REALLY FELT LIFE

WHAT WAS ONE THING YOU SAW OR NOTICED TODAY THAT WAS FULL OF LIFE?

WHERE DO YOU FEEL MOST LIFE IN YOU?

WHAT IS ONE THING THAT YOU WILL LOVE DOING TOMORROW AND LOVE WAKING UP IN THE MORNING TO FACE?

THEMES AND TOPICS FROM *YOUR BEAUTIFUL LIFE*

As we said at the beginning we go through many experiences, stages, moods and emotions in the course of our lives and what follows is a list of these kinds of moods and experiences.

As we also said, you will not find complete answers here for what you are experiencing but rather an invitation and, hopefully, the inspiration to begin to see and handle your experiences and your emotions in new ways.

TEASERS

Anybody who submits correct answers to all of the Teasers in this book to the satisfaction of *Maybe International* will receive a small surprise in recognition.

Brian Smyth

Is a Managing Partner and founder of Maybe International, a Company dedicated to developing a new paradigm of managing and leading and to helping individuals and Companies realise the enormous possibilities in their lives and organisations.

A former NASA and General Motors manager, Brian has over twenty years experience helping organizations and individuals in different parts of the world to achieve new levels of performance, success and well-being.

He is the co-founder of the '**Managing to be Human Forum**' which brings together Company leaders who are searching for a more human and authentic way to manage their organizations. He is the author of the book *Managing to be Human* which explains how it is not only possible to manage in a human way but why that is a better and more effective way to manage.

Brian also helps sports teams and individuals to new levels of performance, achievement and well-being in their particular sports.

Maybe's goal is to make life better for Companies and for the people who work in them. We in Maybe would be very happy to hear from anyone who would like more information on any of the themes spoken of in the book or who would welcome help in any of the areas covered.

Maybe International Ireland
27 Fitzwilliam Square
Dublin 2
Ireland

+353 868 177 114
brian@maybe.ie
www.maybe.ie

Maybe I
Long before that day
Shall sway early one morning at the bridgehead
Where I shall thrust my shadow on the asphalt way.

Maybe I long after that day
On my shaven cheek my stubble turning grey-
Shall remain alive

And I long after that day
(if I've been able to survive)
Shall lean on the side wall of the city squares
On the evening of a holiday and play
The violin to the old-timers
Who survived like myself the last fight.

All around us are the glittering sidewalks
Of a marvelous night and the steps
Of brave new human beings
Singing brave new songs.